MICHIGAN STATE UNIVERSITY
LIBRARY
JUN 3 0 2004

The American Oil Industry

A Failure of Anti-Trust Policy

A study of the structure and operations of the oil industry and the need for immediate and effective anti-trust action published by the Marine Engineers' Beneficial Association, prepared by Stanley H. Ruttenberg and Associates, Inc., Norman Medvin, Senior Consultant.

BUSINESS LIB.

HD
9565
.S76
c.3

Published By

Marine Engineers' Beneficial Association
17 Battery Place, New York, N.Y. 10004

JESSE M. CALHOON, *President*
December, 1973

Prepared for MEBA By

Stanley H. Ruttenberg and Associates, Inc.
1211 Connecticut Avenue, N.W.
Washington, D.C. 20036
Price: $4.00

printed in U.S.A.

FOREWORD

Oil is a major concern of the Marine Engineers' Beneficial Association. A large part of our membership is engaged in transporting oil by ship in the American coastwise trade. But the nation will need to import a growing proportion of our oil supplies in the next two decades, and the transport of these imports can have an exceedingly substantial impact on the members of this union.

It is essential—from the standpoint both of America's national economy and our national defense posture—that this increasing flow of oil and other energy sources be carried in ships carrying the flag of the United States of America. The Marine Engineers' Beneficial Association, like other labor organizations in the maritime field, has been advocating most strongly that a far higher proportion of the international tanker fleet bringing petroleum to the United States should consist of American ships with American crews. We are determined to continue working toward that objective.

Our increasing preoccupation with the import problem has led directly to this study of the oil industry.

It is of the greatest importance to us to determine how the oil industry reaches its decisions, who makes those decisions, and what are the considerations that influences them.

Are we dealing with individual companies, with a group of companies, or with outside masters?

On a broader plane, in terms of the nation's general welfare, to whom do we look when we speak of an energy crisis?

Are the conditions into which we have drifted the result of happenstance or are they the culmination of a well-ordered design?

If there is more design than happenstance, to whom do we look to improve the situation . . . and how do we go about it?

To answer these questions, the Marine Engineers' Beneficial Association commissioned the services of a prestigious economic consulting firm—Stanley H. Ruttenberg & Associates of Washington, D.C. Mr. Ruttenberg was U.S. Manpower Administrator in the Kennedy Administration and an Assistant Secretary of Labor in the Johnson Administration. His firm produced this study, which,

I think, will become part of the basic library of reference tools used to analyze restrictive combinations and structural control in the oil industry.

The study demonstrates what many of us have long suspected: There is a hard core of joint action and control in the oil industry surrounded at its periphery by semi-independent fiefdoms which offer a somewhat deceptive patina of truly independent competition. The study reveals the multiple ties within the oil industry, in what may be a flagrant disregard of the spirit and specific application of the antitrust laws. Furthermore, the study spotlights the harmony in which the oil industry operates—and puts the harsh light of disclosure on the industry's policy of acquiring competing forms of energy. I find it shocking that U.S. officialdom has permitted the high officials of the oil companies to skirt the legality of the antitrust laws; these powerful men have never been seriously challenged in the one area where even modest enforcement would do the most good: the power of control.

We in MEBA are very pleased to have initiated this study. I commend its findings to the government regulatory agencies, the Congress and the public at large.

Jesse M. Calhoon, *President*
Marine Engineer's Beneficial Association

TABLE OF CONTENTS

APPENDIX

LIST OF TABLES

CHARTS

I. PURPOSE OF THE STUDY

The purpose of this presentation is to focus attention on certain economic and financial practices of the oil industry which may be anticompetitive or otherwise in violation of the spirit, if not the letter, of the nation's antitrust laws. Its main thrust is to show that popularly held assumptions about vigorous competition in the oil industry are false.

These possible anticompetitive practices take many forms and any single one may be obscured in the vastness of the arena in which the firms in this industry operate. Indeed it is their global scope of operations, coupled with less than an ardent passion for revealing details, which gives the oil industry the ability to fragmentize and conceal its endeavors so that no single coordinated picture can be drawn of its mammoth affairs.

Always an industry of the first magnitude of importance, it has assumed an even larger role today. "Energy crisis" is a phrase of national concern and it will be shown that the oil industry and the energy industry are virtually synonymous.

It appears evident, on the basis of available data, that the oil industry's objectives are not one and the same with an advancement of the general welfare. Its willfulness, intense self interest, concentration of control, opportunities for anticompetitive practice, favored industry status and economic and political power mark it as one of the last outposts of swashbuckling enterprise.

Questionable Behavior

Under the guise of "lack of incentive", it seeks to wring more concessions from an already generous government. It is contended by some jurists and economists that the oil industry, through the proliferation of the joint venture and its ties with the financial community, certainly violates the spirit of the antitrust laws. The industry constantly threatens the peace of mind of the American public with cries of "shortage" at the same time that it threatens a sit-down strike with respect to exploration for new supplies. It sup-

1

plicates for additional profits as it cynically pockets a depletion allowance and enjoys loopholes on earnings around the world. It carefully maximizes its investments in petroleum and gas energy resources at the same time that it coincidentally is awarded the bulk of the research funds to find substitutes for petroleum and gas. Not content with its own vertical integration in which it controls the oil industry from the extraction of crude to its refining, transmission and marketing, it now has reached out to acquire control of competing forms of energy resources such as uranium and coal. Through the caprice of energy resource distribution around the world, it is in a good position today to contribute weight to the foreign policy of the United States.

Reason for Concern

In normal times such behavior might excite only an elitist fringe. Today, with the energy crisis around the corner, if not immediately at hand, the concern touches every citizen. Our reliance on imported crude and liquefied natural gas within the immediate future is a grim reality.

If the oil industry's practices in any way restrict the availability of its products, further the inflationary spiral and endanger the national interest, the question is whether we can permit the interests of a single industry to be placed above the general welfare.

What can and must be done to realign the behavior of the oil industry is a problem for the investigatory function of government, the regulatory functions of the Federal Trade Commission, the Interstate Commerce Commission and the Federal Power Commission, the antitrust powers of the Department of Justice and the Federal Trade Commission, and for an aroused community who will have to pay hundreds of millions, if not billions, of dollars in higher prices for petroleum and its derivitives.

If the price of a single gallon of gasoline rose by one penny, the cost to American motorists would be almost $1 billion. It is already evident that gasoline will rise about six cents a gallon and that cost per year would be a staggering $6 billion to motorists alone.

The cost of a gallon of gas to the consumer can be reduced to dollars and cents. What about the major intangibles, as for example the impact on American foreign policy? The State Department will inexorably be drawn into world-wide oil negotiations, either officially or sub-rosa.

What of the enormous outflow of American dollars to the sandy shores of the Persian Gulf? The Treasury Department and indeed the entire world's monetary experts will place this high on their calendar of priorities. The problem is far too important to be left to a handful of international oil cartels.

We are on the brink of major changes in the manner in which we conduct our oil and energy policies. Increasing import quotas, shipping liquefied natural gas in new types of vessels, producing electricity by nuclear energy, and converting coal into petroleum and natural gas are already making an impact. Enticing the sheikhs to invest their surplus funds in American oil refining, pipeline and marketing ventures—sort of giving them a stake in private enterprise —and perhaps in so doing to increase the international oil cartel to eight or nine members from the current seven, may be another innovative approach to this viscous dilemma. It is obvious that while always looking to precedence, either in the courts, in administrative decisions, or in established corporate practices, we cannot entirely rely on the old manner of doing things.

History of Major Antitrust Actions

The history of antitrust litigation in the oil industry is a full and continuing one. Many approaches have been used over the years to pin the label of monopoly on the oil industry. Some were conspicuously successful as, for example, the breakup of the Standard Oil Trust in 1911. Others had a patina of success in that the courts ruled against the companies but the latter were able to circumvent the rules by various stratagems. For example, the companies stoutly maintained that the gasoline dealer had the legal right to sell more than one type of gasoline, although in practice he was tied to a single supplier. At the other end of the spectrum there were a number of court actions which were either a stand-off where no actions were taken or ones in which the petroleum companies successfully defended themselves. The "Mother Hubbard" case in 1940, one of the most comprehensive suits filed by the government, ignored the approach of segmenting the industry into its four divisions (production, transportation, refining, and marketing).

The keystone of antitrust laws began in 1890 with the Sherman Act. It said that "every contract, combination, in the form of trust or otherwise, or conspiracy, in restraint of trade or commerce among the several states, or with foreign nations, is declared to be illegal". It sought to wipe out the power over men's lives—as well as the economy—exercised by the trust.

In 1914, Congress recognized that economic power in and of itself was a thing to fear. The Clayton Act was designed to prevent the acquisition of monopoly power, not merely its abuse. Some of its provisions were:

(1) It shall be unlawful for any person engaged in commerce, in the course of such commerce, either directly or indirectly, to discriminate in price between different purchasers of commodities of like grade and quality, where either or any of the purchases involved in such discrimination are in commerce, where such commodities are sold for use, consumption, or resale within the United States and where the effect of such discrimination may be substantially to lessen competition or tend to create a monopoly in any line of commerce. . . .

(2) No corporation engaged in commerce shall acquire directly or indirectly the whole or any part of the stock or other share capital, and no corporation subject to the jurisdiction of the Federal Trade Commission shall acquire the whole or any part of the assets of another corporation engaged also in commerce, where in any line of commerce in any section of the country, the effect of such acquisition may be substantially to lessen competition, or to tend to create a monopoly.

(3) No person at the same time shall be a director in any two or more corporations, any of which has capital surplus and undivided profits aggregating more than $1 million, engaged in whole or in part in commerce, if such corporations are or shall have been competitors, so that the elimination of competition by agreement between them would constitute a violation of any other provisions of any of the antitrust laws.

In 1950, Congress reiterated its intent to prevent concentration brought about by mergers which tend to substantially lessen competition or to create a monopoly in any line of commerce in any section of the country.

There is considerable interest today in the monopoly area and particularly in the oil industry and related energy fields.

Senator Hart introduced, on July 24, 1972, a bill entitled "The Industrial Reorganization Act", a purpose of which was to supplement the antitrust laws. This bill places emphasis on vertical and horizontal aspects of concentration as well as other approaches.

The Select Committee on Small Business of the House of Representatives, 92nd Congress, first session, has made a study on the "Concentration by Competing Raw Fuel Industries in the Energy Market and its Impact on Small Business". This study was completed in December 1971, and requested specific action on the part of various government agencies.

The Justice Department, partly as a result of prodding by the Small Business Committee and partly on its own accord, is active in several areas. They are investigating joint venture petroleum pipelines, including the proposed Trans-Alaska pipeline system. They have also initiated other investigations into various aspects of operations of the fuel and energy industries which, they claim, it is premature to discuss at this time.

A Federal Trade Commission study by its Bureau of Economics, presumably because of its assignment by the Small Business Committee, will focus on oil company and conglomerate participation in the energy market. There will be two studies, the first on concentration of production and the second on concentration of reserves. These studies will probably not be available before the end of 1973.

Hearings have been held before the Senate Subcommittee on Antitrust and Monopoly in the 92nd Congress, second session, on "Marketing Practices in the Gasoline Industry."

The Senate Subcommittee on Antitrust and Monopoly, 91st Congress, first session, conducted hearings on the petroleum industry under the general title of "Governmental Intervention in the Market Mechanism".

The Federal Trade Commission, on November 7, 1972, accused Phillips and Sohio of anti-competitive and unfair marketing practices in what may be the first of similar actions against other companies.

The Federal Trade Commission has served notice as recently

as the end of 1972, that its considers it illegal for a director to serve
on the boards of two competing companies even if they seem to be
selling different products. They say a competitor includes not only
companies making identical products, but also those making different products that are competitive. Specifically, the FTC contends
that directorships on the boards of the Aluminum Company of
America and Armco constitute an interlock. Even though the companies are in different industries—aluminum and steel—the FTC
says they compete in such markets as industrial buildings, siding
and auto bumpers. Does this have particular significance for the
oil industry? There are a number of directors who sit on the boards
of competing energy companies, such as pipelines and utilities along
with their service in an oil company. Are not these competing forms
of products? Moreover, the stakes in these interlocks appear far
more substantive that those of the Alcoa-Armco interlock over
which the FTC became so exercised.

It should be recognized that any leadership coming from the Attorney General's office and indeed from some other government agencies is most likely to be desultory. Both the Small Business Committee and Senator Hart have faulted the Department of Justice because of its laggard approach to antitrust action. As an illustration of the poor climate which exists today, not a single top executive of the international, integrated oil companies appeared to testify before the Small Business Committee, each one giving some excuse for his unavailability. The most important official to testify was the president of Humble Oil, one of the subsidiaries of Exxon. In 1939, on the other hand, when the Temporary National Economic Committee was investigating monopoly, all top executives appeared. The committee was armed with subpoena power, but probably more important, the climate of opinion in 1939 was vastly different and the investigation had the support of the incumbent Administration.

Focus of This Report

We have attempted in the following text to show in perhaps a dozen ways how the oil industry acts in concert to pursue its business objectives. The industry does not act in an organized formal structure. In fact, its characteristics are that it is loosely organized and informal. Management no longer sits in a small room and conspires. At least this report cannot prove that such actions take place. Nevertheless, the structure emerges clearly enough.

No less effective, in our judgment, are the myriad relationships which exist among the oil companies and especially among the seven integrated oil companies, all of which can be built into a structured pattern based on concentration of control, interlocking directorates, financial services, joint ventures, professional conformity, reciprocal favors, commonality of interest or "conscious parallelism", long time friendships, and at its worst greed and arrogance.

Can a Nations that runs on oil afford itself the luxury of permitting a corporate elite to determine, or threaten, how the Nation's wheels of industry should run and how its State Department should act abroad?

The facts presented in subsequent sections, while not clothed in legal rhetoric, provide a series of economic and organizational facts upon which to build an inquiry by legitimate sources of investigative power. This could involve the Congress, one or more of the regulatory agencies, a union, or spirited citizen groups.

Fact finding is a precursor to antitrust laws. A fundamental purpose is to subject the activities of the oil industry, representing a great concentration of economic power, to the spotlight of publicity. Such fact finding can prevent the abuse of power. It has been the basic philosophy of the United States as demonstrated in its history of antitrust activity, to oppose vast monopolistic concentrations of power. The contents of this report is a building block which will hopefully point the way to further investigation and action.

II. BASIC FACTS ABOUT THE OIL INDUSTRY

Petroleum and its products is one of the largest industries in the world. It is concerned with discovering and taking crude oil from the earth, transporting the oil from wells to refineries, transporting the refined products from refineries to sales outlets, and in the case of gasoline, operating retail outlets.

Over the years the trend has been for the larger oil companies to become fully integrated, meaning that they are engaged in all four levels of the industry: mining, refining, transportation and marketing. They own the oil fields both in the United States and around the world, control fleets of tankers, operate networks of pipelines, and build and operate refineries and various distribution facilities, including chains of retail gasoline stations.

The major oil companies as a group, refine more crude than they produce and thus depend upon small independent producers for part of their supplies. They may produce more gasoline than they sell at retail and thus, depend upon independent marketing operators to help dispose of their output.

The U.S. Oil Industry

The oil industry in the United States is concentrated among a relatively few huge industrial combines. The first 21 in size are all billion dollar sales companies (Table 1). Seven of the first sixteen largest U.S. industrial firms are integrated oil companies. Four of the seven were created from the old Standard Oil Trust—Exxon, Mobil, Standard of California and Standard of Indiana. Texaco and Gulf are the so-called independents and Shell is a subsidiary of the world-wide Anglo-Dutch combine, Royal Dutch/Shell.

Exxon is by far the most majestic of them all, with sales of almost $19 billion and at least twice as large as its nearest competitor in size, the Mobil Oil Company. (Note: Exxon and Standard Oil of New Jersey are used interchangeably throughout this report. The company was in the process of changing its name and research references referred to both depending on the point of time.)

The five largest oil companies in the United States earned over $4 billion in profits in 1971 alone. The next 25 largest oil companies earned $2 billion in profits (Table 1).

Table 1. Oil Company Sales and Income
30 Largest American Companies, 1971

Company	Sales (Millions)	Net Income (Millions)	Net Income as % of:	
			Sales	Stock-holders Equity
Total (30 companies)	$84,129	$6,038	7.2	—
Exxon	18,701	1,462	7.8	12.6
Mobil	8,243	541	6.6	11.2
Texaco	7,529	904	12.0	13.4
Gulf	5,904	561	9.5	10.2
Standard California	5,143	511	9.9	10.4
Standard Indiana	4,054	342	8.4	9.6
Shell Oil	3,892	245	6.3	8.7
Atlantic Richfield	3,135	199	6.3	6.9
Continental Oil	3,051	109	3.6	7.1
Tenneco	2,841	184	6.5	10.9
Occidental	2,400	(67)[1]	—	—
Phillips	2,363	132	5.6	7.6
Union Oil	1,981	115	5.8	7.4
Sun Oil	1,939	152	7.8	8.8
Cities Service	1,810	105	5.8	7.7
Ashland Oil	1,614	24[1]	1.5	5.3
Standard Ohio	1,394	55	3.9	5.2
Amerada Hess	1,349	133	9.9	24.0
Getty Oil	1,343	131	9.7	9.2
Signal Companies	1,273	29	2.2	4.6
Marathon	1,183	68[1]	4.1	8.2
Kerr-McGee	603	41	6.7	10.7
Diamond Shamrock	573	25	4.4	6.8
Universal Oil	442	(27)[1]	—	—
American Petrofina	275	13	4.8	9.6
Clark Oil	267	4	1.3	4.6
Commonwealth Oil	256	16	6.3	9.5
Lubrizol	198	23	11.8	18.7
Parker-Hannifin	194	7	3.5	9.2
Crown Central Petroleum	179	1	.4	1.5

[1] Extraordinary charge of at least 10% of income shown.
Source: Fortune Magazine's Directory of 500 Largest Corporations.

Net income on the sales dollar was 7.2 percent. The largest integrated oil companies, because of their very profitable investments abroad, had a somewhat larger return on sales than did the other companies operating primarily in the domestic market.

Reflecting their huge investment in plant and equipment, oil companies capture 8 of the first 10 places with the largest amount of assets per employee—between $155,000 and $400,000 per person.

World Oil Production

Oil production around the world in 1971 totalled 17.7 billion barrels. Of this amount, one-fifth was produced in the United States and almost two-fifths in the Middle East. The other substantive producers consisted of the USSR and its eastern European neighbors with 16%, and Venezuela, 7% (Table 2 and Chart I).

To understand the unfolding drama in oil, however, is to look not only at current production and its distribution but also at the distribution of the world's proven oil reserves. An examination of these reserves reveals an altogether different pattern.

Now it is seen that a capricious nature has concentrated an enormous pool of oil around the Persian Gulf. The Middle East accounts for no less than 58% of the world's proven oil reserves as of the close of 1971. Africa accounts for another 9%, so that together the Arab-Muslim world controls two-thirds of the world's known oil supplies. The Communist countries, virtually all Russia, account for another 15% of the world's proven reserves (Table 3).

On the other hand the total Western Hemisphere commands some 13% of the reserves, half of which is attributed to the United States. This distribution carries with it the seed of development of a major aspect of American foreign policy over the next several decades.

Although the distribution of world reserves has created an entirely new geographical pattern of availability, the future consumption of oil is most likely to retain its current characteristics, namely, that the bulk of the demand will continue to exist in the highly industrialized places like the United States, Western Europe, a small portion of the USSR, and Japan. The United States in 1971 was estimated to consume 30% of total world needs. Credit Western

11

Table 2. World Oil Production, 1930-71
(Millions of Barrels)

Year	USA	Venezuela	USSR[1]	Kuwait	Saudi Arabia	Iran	Iraq	Libya	Trucial Oman[2]	World	USA as Percent of World
1930	898	137	126	—	—	46	1	—	—	1,374	63.6
1935	997	148	182	—	—	57	27	—	—	1,655	60.2
1940	1,353	186	219	—	5	66	24	—	—	2,150	62.9
1945	1,714	323	149	—	21	131	35	—	—	2,595	66.0
1950	1,974	547	266	126	200	242	50	—	—	3,803	51.9
1955	2,484	787	510	398	352	121	251	—	—	5,626	44.2
1960	2,575	1,042	1,184	594	450	391	355	—	—	7,913	36.1
1965	2,849	1,275	1,931	798	748	700	483	443	103	11,317	25.2
1970	3,517	1,353	2,729	1,090	1,387	1,397	570	1,209	283	16,690	21.1
1971	3,454	1,295	2,911	1,167	1,742	1,662	624	1,008	387	17,653	19.6

[1] USSR includes Eastern Germany, Poland, Czechoslovakia, Roumania, Bulgaria, and Albania.
[2] Trucial Oman includes Abu Dhabi and Dubai.

Source: 1930-1955 Petroleum Press Service; 1960-1970 Statistical Abstract of United States; 1971 Department of Interior.

Chart I   U.S. Oil Production

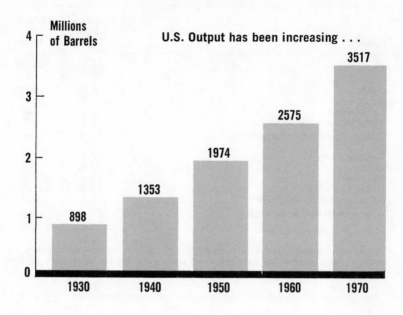

Millions of Barrels

U.S. Output has been increasing . . .

4
3517
3
2575
2
1974
1353
1
898
0
1930   1940   1950   1960   1970

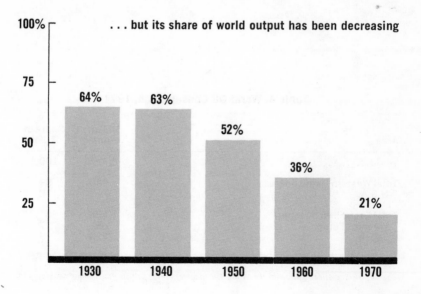

100%   . . . but its share of world output has been decreasing

75
64%   63%
52%
50
36%
25
21%
1930   1940   1950   1960   1970

Table 3. World "Published Proved" Oil Reserves, 1971

Country	Thousand Million Tons	Share of Total
World	87.0	100.0%
U.S.A.	5.9	6.8
Canada	1.3	1.5
Caribbean	2.4	2.8
Other Western Hemisphere	2.0	2.3
Total Western Hemisphere	11.6	13.4
Western Europe	2.7	2.3
Africa	7.8	8.9
Middle East	50.1	57.6
USSR, Eastern Europe	13.4	15.4
Other Eastern Hemisphere	2.1	2.4
Total Eastern Hemisphere	75.4	86.6

Source: BP Statistical Review of the World Oil Industry, 1971, British Petroleum Company, Ltd.
NOTE: Proved oil reserves are those which have been located and can be efficiently extracted with existing techniques.

Table 4. World Oil Consumption, 1971

Area	Million Tons	Share of Total
World	2,396	100%
Total Western Hemisphere	940	39
U.S.A.	715	30
Total Eastern Hemisphere	1,456	61
Western Europe	652	27
Japan	220	9

Source: BP Statistical Review of the World Oil Industry, 1971, British Petroleum Company, Ltd.

Europe with 27% and Japan another 9%, and you continue to have a picture, prospectively, of the major importing areas around the world (Table 4).

Future Energy Demand in the United States

From the comparison of United States oil production (533 million tons) and consumption (715 million tons) in 1971, it is clear that the United States is already a shortage Nation in the petroleum market. This imbalance is expected to grow in magnitude. Official U.S. Treasury estimates of the shortfall, the latter tantamount to the volume of imports, is shown in Chart II.

Projections over the next 15 years reveal that the U.S.A. is expected to consume more than double the amount of oil that it used in 1970. While some of this will undoubtedly be taken up by further exploration and by availability from Alaska's North Slope and the Gulf of Mexico, there is no doubt that the shortage will grow larger with each passing year. Significantly, U.S. dependence on oil, relatively, will grow larger rather than smaller, despite its continuing domestic scarcity. Studies show that estimated consumption of the five sources of primary energy will give oil a larger role in 1985, relatively, than it enjoyed in 1970. Whereas oil consumption in the United States accounted for 44.6% of all sources of energy in 1970, it is estimated that this proportion will increase to 47.4% by 1985 (Table 5.)

Table 5. Future Consumption of Sources of Primary Energy

Energy	Thousands of Barrels Daily (Oil Equivalent)		
	1970	1985	% Change
Oil	14,709	30,170	+105%
Natural Gas	10,417	12,830	+ 23
Coal	6,497	10,555	+ 62
Water Power	1,247	1,805	+ 45
Nuclear	110	8,355	+660
Total	32,980	63,715	+ 93

Source: Outlook for Energy in the U.S. to 1985, Chase Manhattan Bank, 1972.

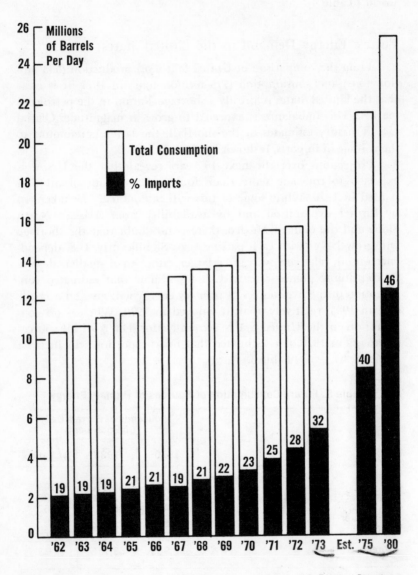

Chart II
American Oil Consumption

26 — Millions of Barrels Per Day

Total Consumption

% Imports

'62 '63 '64 '65 '66 '67 '68 '69 '70 '71 '72 '73 Est. '75 '80

19 19 19 21 21 19 21 22 23 25 28 32 40 46

Source: U.S. Treasury Department

Although the greatest percentage growth in usage is anticipated for nuclear energy, the relatively modest progress thus far, the cost overruns in nuclear plants coming on stream, technical difficulties, and vigorous resistance by ecologists have slowed this development in the past and may make future projections for this energy form far too rosy. On the other hand, a crash emphasis on the gasification and liquefaction of coal may also alter future patterns considerably.

Seven International Oil Companies of the Free World

U.S. oil companies lost no time in moving outside of the United States in their search for oil. Mexico, South Ameirca, the Persian Gulf, North Africa and the North Sea, generally speaking, were the sequences in which the oil industry expanded its feverish quest for new discoveries. Three progeny of the old Standard Oil Trust, two European combines—Royal Dutch/Shell and British Petroleum (nee Anglo-Persian and then Anglo-Iranian), and two major independents in the United States—Texaco and Gulf—most aggressively exploited the worldwide search. As a result, there were born seven major international integrated oil companies who among them amassed the major portion of the oil wealth of the non-communist world.

These seven companies, and an eighth—the Compagnie Francaise Des Petrolles—were reported in 1966 to control 62% of the world's crude petroleum runs and 58% of refining capacity (excluding North America and Communist countries).[1] These companies, through a vast network of interlocking enterprises as well as hundreds of subsidiaries each, are masters of the oil world. Advertisements by a major integrated oil company in the United States presenting the viewpoint that "43,141 companies have a monopoly on the U.S. oil business" is nothing more than cynical claptrap. The same ad goes on to point out that from this number was omitted some 220,000 service stations which are operated by "independent businessmen" (our quotes). Thus, in one editorial flight of fancy, the miniscule and harassed independent gas station re-

---

[1] M. A. Adelman, The World Petroleum Market, 1972, published for Resources for the Future, Inc.

tailer on the neighborhood corner has been given status with the giant international operators.

Within the last decade or so, the Middle Eastern and some South American countries have become increasingly militant, adopting nationalist policies which have resulted in an assumption of greater ownership of the concessions being operated by the international oil companies. Additionally, they have begun to raise prices on their output. The oil companies, whether in protective reaction against the possible expropriation by the Arabic countries, or through a natural rapacity for acquisition, have begun to shift their strategies. Since the beginning of the 60's, these major companies began to acquire and control the development of competing energy sources such as coal, uranium, and natural gas. Today they account for upwards of a fifth of U.S. coal production, a significant proportion of the uranium, mining and milling capacity, and of course the predominant share of natural gas production in this country. To make the cycle complete, they also have a stranglehold on the experimentation for the conversion of coal, our most abundant natural energy resource, to liquefied petroleum and natural gas.

So much for a brief economic background of the players in the oil industry. Clearly, the stakes in the oil game are huge. The history of the oil industry is one in which management has not been reluctant to use its vast economic power to influence men and whole nations. In a world where countries frequently stand on quicksand, the oil industry has provided a continuity which is the envy of politicians and historians.

Is this continuity an accident, a chance occurrence? Not at all. The overt steps which the industry has taken are far too purposeful to permit a conclusion of arms-length relationships. We will show in the following pages how the oil industry, working in a general climate of forbearance in the United States, has been able to wield its power, sometimes malevolently, most frequently in its self interest, to maintain control and to create the opportunities for joint behavior which could provide the framework for actions against the general welfare.

III. CONTROL OF COMPETING ENERGY SOURCES

Within the past decade there has been a growing trend toward concentration of ownership in the energy market. Oil companies have been actively acquiring coal and uranium reserves and production capacity.

Further the major oil companies are acquiring oil shale and tar sands, as well as water rights, in many areas of the country. The extent and significance of acquisitions of oil shale by oil companies do not appear available even for preliminary analysis. The federal government owns about 80 percent of the oil shale lands (11,000,000 acres concentrated in three western states). Oil shale and tar sands are potential sources of energy which at the present time are not technologically convertible to energy on a competitive basis (Table 6).

This growing concentration in the fuel maket is unprecedented in the history of the United States. A relatively small number of oil companies, not content to own a vast portion of the oil reserves in the United States have now branched out to acquire competing energy forms. The major oil companies account for approximately 84% of U.S. refining capacity; about 72% of the natural gas production and reserve ownership; 30% of the domestic coal reserves and some 20% of the domestic coal production capacity; and over 50% of the uranium reserves and 25% of the uranium milling capacity.[2] (Chart III)

One needs to look very closely in our history to find equivalent parallels of such a broad-ranging control of our natural resources.

---

[2] Concentration by Competing Raw Fuel Industries in the Energy Market and Its Impact on Small Business, Subcommittee on Special Small Business Problems, House of Representatives, 92nd Congress, 1972.

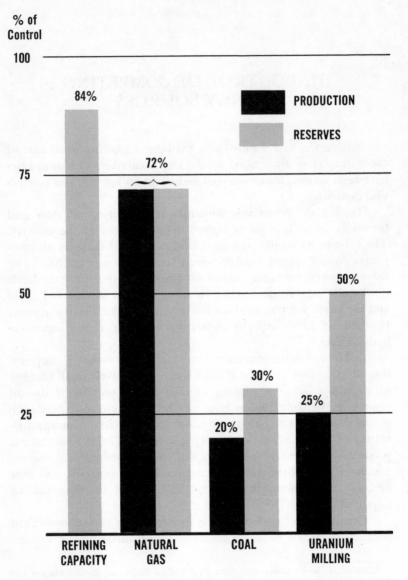

Chart III. Oil Industry Control of Competing Energy Resources
United States, 1970

% of
Control

■ PRODUCTION

▨ RESERVES

Source: Small Business Committee, 92nd Congress, 1971

The oil companies, not content with reaching out in vertical fashion to control the industry from the mining of crude petroleum through the refining, transportation and marketing process, are now acquiring competing sources of energy. In other words, the oil industry has not only achieved vertical integration but is in the process of acquiring horizontal integration of its competitors.

The Clayton Act of 1914 appears to be definitive on the negative aspects of such acquisitions. It says "No corporation engaged in commerce shall acquire directly or indirectly the whole or any part of the stock or other share capital, and no corporation subject

Table 6. Diversification In The Energy Industries By The 25 Largest Petroleum Companies, Ranked By Assets, 1970

Petroleum Company	Rank In Assets	Energy Industry				
		Gas	Oil Shale	Coal	Uranium	Tar Sands
Standard Oil (New Jersey)..	1	X	X	X	X	X
Texaco	2	X	X	X	X	
Gulf	3	X	X	X	X	X
Mobil	4	X	X		X	
Standard Oil of California...	5	X	X			
Standard Oil (Indiana)	6	X	X		X	X
Shell	7	X	X	X	X	X
Atlantic Richfield	8	X	X	X	X	X
Phillips Petroleum	9	X	X		X	X
Continental Oil	10	X	X	X	X	
Sun Oil	11	X	X	X	X	X
Union Oil of California	12	X	X		X	
Occidental [1]	13	X		X		
Cities Service	14	X	X		X	X
Getty [2]	15	X	X		X	
Standard Oil (Ohio) [3]	16	X	X	X	X	
Pennzoil United, Inc.	17	X			X	
Signal	18	X				
Marathon	19	X	X			
Amerada-Hess	20	X			X	
Ashland	21	X	X	X	X	
Kerr-McGee	22	X		X	X	
Superior Oil	23	X	X			
Coastal States Gas Producing	24	X				
Murphy Oil	25	X				

[1] Includes Hooker Chemical Company.
[2] Includes Skelly and Tidewater.
[3] Includes reported British Petroleum assets.
Source: National Economic Research Association, Washington, D. C.

to the jurisdiction of the FTC shall acquire the whole or any part of the assets of another corporation engaged also in commerce, where in any line of commerce in any section of the country, the affect of such acquisition may be substantially to lessen competition, or to tend to create a monopoly."

We believe, and the Select Committee on Small Business of the House of Representatives also believes, that the oil industry may be in violation of this law.

This growing concentration in the fuel market could result in the following:

1. A dwindling of available fuel supplies, because oil companies will schedule their production to best meet the needs of their internal situations.
2. The maintenance of artificially high price levels. Highly concentrated industries tend to insulate themselves from outside competitive forces and maintain high prices which are rigid and less responsive to economic change.
3. Reduction in the number of competitors through acquisition, merger or bankruptcy.
4. Substitutability of competing fuels may be foreclosed through concentration of control.
5. Research in the substitutability of fuels, namely liquefaction and gasification of coal, could be retarded if the oil companies through their coal subsidiaries are given large contracts to do the required research.

COAL

Coal mining, the besooted, disease-laden and hazard-prone industry of post-World War II, suddenly achieved glamour status in the early 1960's. Until then reduced productivity, loss of market, declining profitability and glowing predictions for nuclear-powered electric generating facilities caused forecasts of economic doom for the coal industry. Instead the reverse happened. Sharply increased demand for electric generating power in a burgeoning U.S. economy, coupled with a failure of nuclear power to be developed in accordance with a too optimistic time table, and the growing prospect of coal substitutability suddenly gave the coal industry an attractive aura.

The oil industry, quick to recognize the potential demand for coal, both in terms of existing requirements and future conversion to oil and gas, began to acquire coal reserves and production capacity. The first major acquisition occurred in 1963, when Gulf Oil absorbed the Pittsburgh and Midway Coal Company. The movement picked up considerable momentum when the Department of Justice in 1966 concluded that Continental Oil's purchase of Consolidation Coal Company, accounting for fully 11% of the Nation's coal production, warranted no antitrust action. The tortured logic of the Justice Department in approving this acquisition most probably set in motion a spate of activity on the part of other oil companies to acquire coal reserves and producing mines. Today, two of the three largest coal producers are oil companies, five of the largest ten are oil companies, and seven of the largest fifteen are oil firms. Of the top fifteen coal producers only three are independent companies. Based on 1971's national coal tonnage produced, the oil industry now accouts for some 20% of the Nation's coal output (Table 7).

Table 7. Extent of Oil Industry Control of Coal Production, 1971

Acquiring Firm	Acquired Firm	Acquired Firm % Of Market	Date of Acquisition
Gulf Oil.................	Pittsburgh & Midway Coal..	1.3%	1963
Continental Oil.........	Consolidation Coal.........	9.9	1966
Occidental Petroleum..	Island Creek Coal..........	4.1	1968
Standard Oil Ohio......	Old Ben Coal...............	1.9	1968
Ashland Oil [1]...........	Arch Mineral...............	1.1 [2]	1968
Eastern Gas & Fuel.....	Eastern Associated Coal...	2.1	1969-70
Total.............	....	20.4%	

[1] In conjunction with Hunt interests.
[2] 1972 tonnage.

Source: Small Business Committee, 92nd Congress. Production data from Keystone Coal Industry Manual.

Coal Reserves

At least as important as the amount of current production controlled by the oil industry is the extent of coal reserves in oil industry hands. It is estimated that there are 3,210 billion tons of coal reserves,[3] although a relatively small proportion of that is currently minable under present technology. Today, the traditional coal producers are no longer necessarily the big owners of reserves (and what may matter most in the future is how much of these reserves is in low-sulphur coal).

Exxon's Monterey Coal is estimated to possess 7 billion tons of usable reserves today. Continental Oil's Consolidation Coal is assessed at 8 billion tons of usable coal reserves. Occidental's Island Creek Coal is reported to contain 3 billion tons of coal reserves and Pittsburgh and Midway a similar amount. Altogether, seven oil companies own 26 billion tons of the Nation's estimated reserves (Table 8).

Antitrust Illogic

The antitrust division of the Justice Department did not attack the Consolidation Coal-Continental Oil merger on the grounds that each operated in separate markets and also that both companies are not significant potential competitors. This myopic view concerned itself more with the trees than the forest.

Consolidation Coal is one of the largest grantees of experimental monies by the Office of Coal Research, U.S. Department of the Interior, in the gasification of coal. That certainly has national implications, regardless of the area in which Continental Oil operates.

Still a third maxim, is the broad-gage approach of the Clayton Act, which looks with suspicion upon the acquisition by one industry of a competing industry where, even though the products are physically different, they compete with one another in the same (energy) market.

Another concern in the acquistion of coal reserves by the oil industry: the possibility exists that oil companies controlling vast coal reserves could be in a position to limit inter-fuel competition by either withholding coal supplies through non-development of

---

3 James Ridgeway, The Last Play, E. P. Dutton & Company, Inc., New York, 1973, p. 205.

Table 8. Estimated Reserves and Production of Coal, by Company, 1971

Company	Estimated Reserves Total (Billion Tons)	Low Sulphur	Production 1971 (Million Tons)
Burlington Northern	11.0	100%	none
Union Pacific	10.0	50+	none
Kennecott Copper (Peabody Coal)	8.7	27	54.8
Continental Coal (Consolidation Coal)	8.1	35	54.8
Exxon (Monterey Coal)	7.0	N.A.	1.2
American Metal Climax (Amax Coal)	4.0	50	12.5
Occidental Petroleum (Island Creek Coal)	3.3	28	22.8
United States Steel	3.0	N.A.	16.6
Gulf Oil (Pitts. & Midway Coal)	2.6	8	7.0
North American Coal	2.5	80	8.8
Reynolds Metal	2.1	95	none
Bethlehem Steel	1.8	N.A.	12.0
Pacific Power & Light	1.6	100	1.7
American Electric Power	1.5	minimal	5.5
Eastern Gas & Fuel Assoc. (Eastern Assoc. Coal)	1.5	33	11.7
Kerr-McGee	1.5	60	minimal
Norfolk & Western RR	1.4	99	none
Utah International	1.3	94	6.8
Westmoreland Coal	1.2	88	8.4
Pittston Company	1+	100	20.1
Montana Power (Western Energy)	1	100	5.1
Standard Oil of Ohio (Old Ben Coal)	.8	minimal	10.5
Ziegler Coal	.8	0	4.0
General Dynamics (Freeman/United Elec.)	.6	0	11.5
Rochester & Pitts. Coal	.3	0	4.3
Carbon Fuel	.1	97	2.6
American Smelting & Refining (Midland Coal)	.1	0	4.0

Source: Forbes, November 15, 1972

coal reserves or delaying the timing of the development of synethetic oil and gas from coal through less than aggressive research efforts.

Consolidation and Monterey together control 15 billion tons of coal reserves. The Congressional Committee said that Humble Oil (Exxon) has opened only one mine. The Committee added that if large energy suppliers such as Humble could substantially change the available supply of fuels, then small fuel suppliers could be competitively disadvantaged since they would be unable to accurately anticipate rapid increases and decreases in market demand.

With respect to delaying the timing of the development of synthetic oil and gas from coal, it is worthy of note that Continental Oil, the recipient of large research grants for coal gasification, has abandoned its experiment in Cresap, West Va., after having received a grant of some $17 million dollars for a pilot plant. It has taken on a new project to reduce the sulphur content of coal.

In summary, we firmly believe that acquisition of a significant proportion of the coal industry by the oil firms constitutes a clear danger of concentration of control. The Justice Department and the Federal Trade Commission can avail themselves of numerous approaches to head off this trend and require only self-motivation to do so.

URANIUM

The importance of uranium to the Nation's energy problem is that it provides the raw material for nuclear power which is expected to increasingly supplant fossil fuel in electric power generation. Although at the present time nuclear energy accounts for a negligible percentage of the Nation's energy output, it is expected that this proportion will increase to about 13 percent by 1985 (See Table 5) and considerably more than that by the end of the century.

The situation with uranium and nuclear energy is the same as with coal, only the trend is further along. Here again, the oil industry is rapidly acquiring the production, reserves and milling capacity of the uranium industry. Again we see the oil industry controlling a very substantial proportion of a competing energy resource, possibly in violation of the Clayton Act.

Certainly from a self-serving point of view, the strategy of the oil industry cannot be faulted. To acquire control directly of the electric power utility industry would require a dollar sum which even the oil companies, rich as they are, would be unable to bring off. What better way then, for only a fractional expenditure of money, to control uranium, the raw material upon which the electric utility industry would depend. With the single-mindedness of a hawk swooping towards its target, the oil industry through its accelerated acquisition of uranium segments, now holds a sharply honed scalpel against the electric utility jugular.

Trend to Vertical Integration

In general the trend is for U.S. oil companies to integrate vertically from mining through construction of nuclear equipment. Hence, oil companies are involved in uranium mining, refining, and in the case of Gulf Oil's subsidiary, Gulf Atomic, in the construction of nuclear power plants.

In 1970, seventeen oil companies accounted for approximately 55% of the drilling and controlled about 48% of the known low-cost uranium reserves, with approximately 28% of the uranium ore processing capacity.[4] In 1967, Atlantic Richfield acquired Nuclear Materials and Gulf Oil acquired General Atomics Division of General Dynamics. In 1968, Getty Oil acquired Nuclear Fuel Services. Of the major oil companies in the uranium business—Exxon, Atlantic Richfield, Continental, Gulf, Getty, Standard of Ohio, Kerr-McGee, and Sun Oil—each have exploration or reserve holdings; six have mining and milling capacity; two have UF6 conversion; five have fuel preparation or fabrication; four have fuel reprocessing; and one owns a reactor.

Again, as with coal, the Subcommittee of the Small Business Committee of the House of Representatives fears that increasing acquisition of uranium reserves and production capacity by oil companies may tend to lessen future inter-fuel competition in the energy market. An oil company dominated nuclear power industry, in the view of this subcommittee, could be anti-competitive and not in the public interest.

The subcommittee also believes that the growing trend toward concentration by oil companies in the uranium industry should be reversed in order to insure the availability of low-cost uranium resources to the electric power industry.

---

[4] Op. cit.

While there is an actual overproduction of uranium at this time, a joint report of the European Nuclear Energy Agency and the International Atomic Energy Agency indicated that supplies will shrink as nuclear power plants increase in number and that by 1975 or 1976, there may be a shortage of uranium.

NATURAL GAS

Natural gas as an energy form provided an estimated 36% of the total energy requirements of the United States. Since in many instances natural gas pools are discovered in conjunction with liquid petroleum resources it is not surprising that the oil industry controls approximately 72% of the Nation's natural gas production and a similar proportion of its reserves.

A considerable amount of the natural gas reserves is located along the Gulf of Mexico and on the North Slope of Alaska. A large amount of natural gas was also discovered in the Middle East and African oil producing countries, but it was burned off because the means of getting it to the consuming countries was non-existent. Recently, however, technological advances made it possible to freeze natural gas. Now, in a liquefied state, large quantities of it are about to be shipped from these producing areas to the heavily industrialized countries of the world. Hundreds of millions of dollars in contracts for the construction of LNG (liquefied natural gas) ships are being let and it will not be long before this form of energy becomes a significant factor in the American market.

There are assertions that a stringency exists in the availability of natural gas in the United States today. The oil industry insists that a lack of economic incentive, namely low prices, is responsible in large measure for the failure to encourage discovery of new supplies. They have been successful in persuading the Federal Power Commission, which governs prices, to grant a rate increase for gas produced in the southern Louisiana area. In 1971, they were successful in pushing through a 30% increase and they are now asking for another 73% escalation.

The problem here is not one so much of vertical integration in violation of the law—the oil companies discovered natural gas fortuitously as they explored for oil. The problem instead is the availability of natural gas and what must be done to satisfy domestic requirements.

Reserves

The public is bombarded today with dire forecasts of natural gas reserves. Strange as it may seem, the U.S. Government does not make independent estimates based on field procedures of these reserves. Instead, it relies on submission of an estimate by the American Gas Association (AGA), the trade body of the natural gas industry. These AGA reserve figures are submitted by the gas producers as evidence of a decrease in gas supplies available to interstate markets.

It is alleged that producers have understated reserves and withheld supplies to create the appearance of shortage and thereby push up prices. Since these estimates are taken into consideration for a variety of purposes such as pricing, national energy policy, importation of liquefied natural gas, tanker subsidies for this importation, etc., why does the Government not institute a regularized and independent reporting system based, if not in whole then certainly on a sampling basis, of its own testing techniques and applications?

In public testimony the American Public Gas Association describes as unconscionable the "cloak of confidentiality" surrounding the compilation, analysis and evaluation of the AGA's natural gas reserve figures. Reliance by the FPC on gas reserve data supplied by the very industry it purports to regulate further highlights the need for a central depository of energy reserve data from which accurate and reliable reserve estimates may be obtained. The House Committee on Small Business indicated that an audit of these reserve figures conducted by the technical staff of the Federal Power Commission "is likely to have been cursory at best".

The Federal Power Commission's continuing use of reserve figures furnished by the natural gas industry serves only to reduce public confidence in the regulatory process and in those who are sworn to protect the public interest. The Federal Power Commission in fact is now conducting for the first time a one-year survey of natural gas reserves, but it is for a one-time, one-year study only. Already it has run into trouble with the industry. The Federal Trade Commission is about to ask the Justice Department to take to court nine out of eleven natural gas producers that have allegedly refused to submit information on gas reserves that was demanded by the Commission under its subpoena powers.[5]

---

[5] New York Times, February 25, 1973.

The purpose of the survey, of course, is mainly twofold. The FTC wants to determine whether natural gas reserve figures published by the American Gas Association tend to understate the facts. In addition, the Commission wants to know whether any such understatement, if it has occurred, has resulted from collusion.

Incentives

In response to oil industry claims that they lack economic incentive to do exploratory work, the fact is that the United States Government has been very generous with the oil industry. In 1971, the 18 largest oil companies in the Nation earned over $10 billion. Of that tremendous sum, they paid only 6.7% of their net income in federal income taxes.

Many of these companies pay additional sums in foreign and local taxes, but few pay proportionally in taxes as much as the American citizen who earns $15 thousand a year.

From "U.S. Oil Week" are some surprising figures on what major oil companies paid to the United States in 1971:

Company	TAX	PERCENT
Exxon	$211,542,000	7.7
Texaco	30,000,000	2.3
Gulf	31,062,000	2.3
Mobil	85,700,000	7.4
Standard (California)	14,000,000	1.6
Standard (Indiana)	63,462,000	14.5
Shell	43,738,000	14.9
Arco	11,115,000	3.8
Phillips	32,734,000	15.0
Sun	41,081,000	17.4
Union (California)	11,750	7.9
Amerada Hess	22,552,000	9.3
Getty	31,585,000	15.1
Conoco	6,240,000	2.1
Cities Service	9,934,000	8.4
Marathon	14,000	6.1
Standard (Ohio)	1,245,000	2.0
Ashland	23,954,000	46.3

Against this background of very generous tax treatment, a number of questions need to be directed to the oil industry. (Note: Since oil firms control 72% of natural gas production and reserves, we are equating the oil industry with the natural gas industry.)

1. In view of the rate increases granted for natural gas to 20¢ in 1968 and to 26¢ in 1971, what has been the impact of this increased incentive on exploration, discovery, and production of natural gas? Consumers are entitled to know what they got in return for paying higher prices.

2. The rate making procedures on which the Federal Power Commission (FPC) makes its decisions need to be examined. In justifying its request for a 45¢ price, the natural gas industry advances the concept of the costs of alternative fuels which are indeed higher. What justification can there be in a regulated industry for gouging the American public at a 45¢ rate when it costs far less to produce, simply because a petroleum equivalent costs more?

3. Why does not the FPC require individual companies to submit their cost and profit data in rate increase cases rather than accepting an industry wide figure? How is it possible to check the validity of the overall figure without the pieces that make it up?

4. Why are oil companies permitted to make rate increase justification on the basis of a single aspect of their operations in one or more corners of the country? Why not base the increase on total profitability of oil company operations? The oil industry is quick to point out that integration in mining, transmission, refining and marketing is their most viable economic concept. Why then, for purposes of pricing, are they permitted to fragmentize their operations?

Despite the most pressing need for close regulation of the natural gas industry, Chairman Nassikas of the Federal Power Commission recently proposed that Congress revoke the FPC's authority to regulate the prices of "new" gas on the interstate market.[6] Control over natural gas prices has been the province of the Federal government since 1938. Such deregulation will undoubtedly cost the consumer many billions of dollars over the next decade alone.

Two previous attempts had been made by the Congress to deregulate gas prices, but they were vetoed by President Truman in 1948 and by President Eisenhower in 1956.

---

[6] Washington Post, April 11, 1973

IV. GASIFICATION AND LIQUEFACTION OF COAL

The Problem

As a result of oil company acquisitions of coal companies, a substantial proportion of the Federally funded research and development of synthetic fuels from coal has come under the corporate umbrella of the oil industry.

The development of synthetic liquids and gas will have a marked affect on competition in the energy market. Substitution of synthetic gas and oil from coal will probably reduce the market for naturally mined oil and gas. It could obsolete hundreds of millions of dollars of refining plants and mining equipment. The threat to the oil industry is real.

Consequently, a fear exists that research and development of the liquefaction and gasification of coal may be retarded where oil companies dominate a segment of the experimentation. Since oil companies might find their huge investments in refining plants and mining equipment obsoleted, the temptation might be present for them to delay such research and development until the sizable capital investments in existing fossil fuel plants are fully amortized.

Background

Domestic oil and gas reserves are being used up faster than we can replace them. Coal is the Nation's most abundant fossil fuel resource, yet it supplies about one fifth of our energy requirements. In fact, coal is being displaced in some markets because of limits on sulfur content which do not meet the requirements of the recent Environmental Act of 1969. Nuclear power development, which was to replace coal in utility markets, is behind schedule. Thus, with the demand for clean fuels rising and tardiness in the substitution of nuclear energy, the conversion of coal into a useful and accept-

Table 9. Office of Coal Research
Contracts for Research on Gasification & Liquefaction of Coal [1]
(Other than joint OCR-AGA program)
1962-1974

Date of Contract Award	Recipient	Amount
1963-1974	FMC Corp. (Coal liquefaction)	$19,332,000
1963-1973	Consolidation Coal, Cresap (low sulphur) [2]	16,606,000
1966-1972	Pittsburgh & Midway Coal (low sulphur)	7,640,000
1963-1971	Bituminous Coal Research, Ft. Lewis (gasification)	3,439,000
1966-1972	Avco Corp. (MHD)	1,942,000
1964-1967	M. W. Kellogg Co.	1,710,000
1966-1969	Gourdine Systems, Inc.	1,000,000
1964-1968	Atlantic Richfield	918,000
1969-1974	University of Utah	844,991
1962-1964	General Electric	750,000
1968-1973	University of Wyoming	613,000
1962-1969	University of Utah	476,000
1962-1969	Ralph M. Parsons Co.	444,000
1965-1968	Milpar, Inc.	364,000
1965-1972	Iowa State University	276,200
1966-1972	West Virginia University	243,149
1967-1968	Stanford Research Inst.	176,000
1966-1968	Franklin Institute	152,923
1962-1963	Montana State College	26,000
1962-1963	Georgia Tech Research Inst.	24,000

[1] Figures taken from OCR Annual Reports. Contracts may have been modified in subsequent years.
[2] Consolidation's Cresap plant was originally engaged in production of high quality gasoline and switched to experiments on low sulphur coal.
Source: Office of Coal Research, U.S. Department of Interior, Annual Reports.

able energy resource has excited the interest of the public and private sectors.

Most of the world's coal is located in North America and China. In the United States, coal is our most abundant natural resource. At current rates of use, there is enough coal to last for 400 years. The specific interest in coal, therefore, stems from the possibility that with applied research, experimentation and pilot operation a way can be found to translate coal into natural gas or liquid petroleum.

Because of the high sulphur content of most of the coal deposits east of the Mississippi, a concomitant problem arises. Not only is there the challenge of meeting fuel requirements for increased electric generating capacity but it is also necessary to utilize environmentally acceptable fuels. Technology which could provide a clean burning fuel gas from coal would facilitate the conservation of our dwindling national gas reserves, promote the development of electric power generating systems, and utilize the Nation's deposits of high sulphur coal.

Although conversion of coal to gas and oil has been discussed in laboratories for a long time, it's probably fair to say that major experimentation supported by public funds started in the early 1960's. Originally, the R&D was funded solely by the Federal Government through awards to private companies. From 1961 through 1973 some $163 million, and in 1974, $52.5 million, were allocated for experimentation by the Congress (Table 9).

Beginning in 1971 the American Gas Association, spokesman for the natural gas industry, agreed for a period of 4 years to contribute one dollar for every two which the government advanced. The 4-year program, devoted almost exclusively to the conversion of coal to gas, is expected to cost $120 million of which AGA will raise one third (Table 10).

The U.S. Bureau of Mines is another major participant in coal experimentation. Their entry is relatively recent and the bulk of

Table 10. Joint Coal Gasification Program
U.S. Office of Coal Research-American Gas Association
February 1973

Recipient	Project	Amount (Add 000's)
Institute of Gas Technology, Chicago	HYGAS Steam Iron	$19,000
Institute of Gas Technology, Chicago	HYGAS Steam Oxygen	22,000
Consolidation Coal, Rapid City, S. D.	HiBTU Gas	20,377
Bituminous Coal Research, Homer City	HiBTU Gas	25,500
Battelle Memorial Institute	Syn-Gas	4,000
Lurgi Process, Scotland		2,500
Applied Technology, Pittsburgh		7,000
Chem Systems	Methanation	2,000
Braun	Evaluation	4,000

their expenditures will involve a pilot plant in Bruceton, Pa. to be operated by a non-public firm or organization.

What is the Experience?

Since the major effort in the development of these synthetic gases and liquids was given to the Office of Coal Research, U.S. Department of the Interior, it is of interest to examine their role in the conduct of that experimentation over the years.

Of the first $94 million allocated in contracts for research on gasification and liquefaction of coal, some $37 million, or 40%, was given in two contracts to Consolidation Coal Company, a subsidiary of Continental Oil. Another contract of some $8 million, or 8%, was given to the Pittsburgh and Midway Coal Company, a subsidiary of Gulf Oil Corporation. A third, and smaller, contract of almost $1 million was awarded to Atlantic Richfield. Thus the oil-controlled coal companies received a little less than half of total dollar awards.

What is the contract experience of the joint OCR-AGA program? It would appear, from the emphasis given this effort, that the main thrust of U.S. Government and private sector research is in the gasification of coal. Of the proposed expenditure of $120 million between 1971-1975, so far the bulk of the research, in terms of dollars, is given to four major projects. Consolidation Coal Company, Rapid City (subsidiary of Continential Oil) was awarded $20 million. The Institute of Gas Technology, Chicago, is in for two major contracts totalling $19 million and $22 million. Rounding out this group is Bituminous Coal Research for $25.5 million. Together, these 4 research projects account for at least 72% of the $120 million scheduled to be spent on the joint program.

Consolidation Coal's activities at Cresap, West Virginia are a matter of record. This program was subject to large cost over-runs, operated only 90 days over a year's period, and was in effect being abandoned for a new project. The Office of Coal Research staunchly maintains that the money was well spent in view of the findings obtained. Consolidation Coal now has a second contract in Rapid City working on Hi BTU gas.

The Institute of Gas Technology, which has two large contracts, has been described by the Office of Coal Research as "a research subsidiary of the American Gas Association." [7]

The major oil companies account for about 72% of the natural gas production and reserve ownership. The role which the oil industry plays in the AGA therefore is obviously substantial. So once again the pattern is repeated. Three of the four major contracts awarded for the gasification of coal are to be concentrated in three firms whose relationship to the oil industry might be interpreted as something less than at arms-length.

Despite Mr. Fumich's specific description of the status of the Institute of Gas Technology, it is contended that the Institute is actually not an officially designated research arm of the AGA. Nevertheless, it is conceded that a very large proportion of the research contracts of the Institute are with the oil and gas industry and it is reasonable to raise a question about the "independence" of that organization.

Competitive Effects

Production of synthetic gasoline is estimated only one or two cents a gallon above the cost of the gasoline refined from fossil crude oil. Synthetic pipeline quality gas is predicted to be competitive with the imported liquified natural gas (there is a major effort under way today to import liquified natural gas from the Middle East and the Mediterranean with hundreds of millions of dollars of investments in the construction of LNG vessels). Low sulphur synthetic crude oil will likely compete with a low sulphur fossil crude oil for use in the production of heating and residual fuel oil. [8]

The competition of synthetic liquids and gas, vis-as-vis the fossil fuel suppliers, would have beneficial effects on the electric power industry, which is becoming dangerously dependent on oil companies for raw fuel supplies to power its generators. Were the electric utilities to become totally dependent upon an all encom-

---

[7] Testimony of George Fumich, Jr., Director of Office of Coal Research, U.S. Department of the Interior, in hearings before the Subcommittee on Special Small Business Problems, House of Representatives, July 20, 1971, Hearings, p. 287.

[8] Summary report of Subcommittee on Special Small Business Problems, 92nd Congress, 1971.

passing oil industry for its supplies of raw fuel, price competition among alternative fuel resources would be eliminated.

If the utilities, which generate electricity and directly compete with fossil fuel in the industrial, commercial and residential markets, were dependent on the price of fuel which oil companies charged them, it would be prey to whatever price the oil and gas interests would charge.

The lack of competitive raw fuel alternatives available to electric utilities could result in higher electric utility bills to the public.

Questions Needing Answers

There is a general consensus in this country that we will be facing an energy crisis before the turn of the century. While enough gas and oil is available from abroad, a growing dependence by this country on foreign output can be a threat to our economic survival. One of the best hopes to reduce this dependence and make the country more self sufficient is to gasify or liquify our huge volume of coal reserves.

Regardless of whether the effort to develop competitive fuels has been enhanced or retarded as a result of an inordinate share of contracts being awarded to oil companies, there is a question of propriety, if indeed not one of national safety, in awarding research contracts to companies which could benefit most from a delay in development of their requisite technology.

Why was a second contract given to Consolidation Coal? It is alleged that Consolidation had one of the finest research teams in the country. What is there in the record of their performance at Cresap that permits the office of Coal Research to repose so much confidence in Consolidation's technical abilities? If other research companies could not have done better, could they have done worse?

Why do three of four major gasification contracts go to research institutions closely allied to the oil and gas industry? Is the scientific base of this country so narrow that competent technicians cannot be found outside of the fossil fuel industries? Contracts awarded to other prestigious groups are small in value and limited in scope.

Must we ask companies whose interest it may be to delay experimentation to take upon themselves the major thrust for that experi-

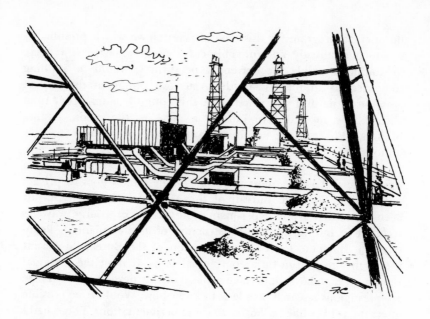

mentation? In other fields of anti-trust legislation we have accepted the concept of the Clayton Act which was designed to prevent the acquisition of monopoly power, not merely its abuse. Applying the same concept here with some modification, why need we chance the possibility of abuse? The stakes are too high to become involved in games of chance.

Why is AGA's participation needed at this stage? Did AGA offer to participate in the first ten years of OCR research? Has the research conducted by OCR over the last 10 years already pointed the way to a successful conclusion and the oil companies now wish to share in a no-risk undertaking? What meaning can the $10 million annual participation by AGA have in the overall view? To small handfuls of oil and gas companies who are investing hundreds of millions of dollars in prospecting for gas in the Gulf of Mexico alone, what is the significance of a paltry $10 million? Is it possible that by this investment the oil companies see a way to acquire proprietary rights even though the Interior Department thinks otherwise?

In view of the so-called energy crisis and the long lead time necessary for construction and operation of pilot plants, why is there not a crash program for this type of research on which presumably so much is already known. This crash program, even if it were to double or triple the current expenditures, would be nothing compared to an increase to the American public in the cost of gasoline or natural gas, whether in this country or imported from abroad. We succeeded in putting a man on the moon, costing billions. Why can we not invest a few tens of millions to *save* billions?

Why not a greater role for government experimentation in this process? To date, most if not all of the money goes to private contractors. The U.S. Bureau of the Mines which has itself just been inserted into the experimentation picture in a large way has received $9 million for the construction of a pilot plant in Pennsylvania. But here to, it is the intention of the Bureau to permit the facility to be run on a contractual basis. Cannot the National Bureau of Standards undertake a piece of this development? These are prestigious research people with know-how. Would it be possible to create a TVA-like authority to do experimentation? These paths would not exclude oil company participation but simply broaden the experimentation base.

These are but a few of the relatively urgent questions which need answers in the near future.

V. JOINT VENTURES AND THE OIL INDUSTRY

In recent decades the oil industry has resorted to a combination device which it has used to reduce the rigor and risks of competition. That device is the joint venture.

A joint venture is basically a company in which the bulk if not all of the stock is owned by two or more parent companies. It represents a separate corporate enterprise and differs from a simple subsidiary which is largely owned by a single firm.

The joint venture is one of the relatively newer techniques that takes its place in the non-competitive valhalla alongside the community of interest, the merger, the consortium, the pool, the trust and the not-so-gentle gentlemen's agreement. Although the Congress and the Department of Justice have taken a tolerant attitude toward the joint venture, perhaps because the Sherman Act does not outlaw it *per se*, it nevertheless opens the door to the most flagrant anti-competitive abuses in our industrial society.

The history of anti-trust activity is replete with attempts to prove collusion. In overlapping directorships and even in secondary overlaps, mere presence of a director on two competing boards is suspicious if not illegal. A measure of illegal competition is the point at which two or more companies are presumed to constitute a danger on the basis of market share. Is it 20%, 40%, the top four with 50%? Is it the geographic market and what is the definition of the market? Parallelism of action, restraint of trade and foreclosure are a few among other doctrines of antitrust procedures. The instances of approaches to the problem of anti-trust are as complex, devious, esoteric and ingenious as they are numerous.

The joint venture, on the other hand, appears to be a simplistic, bold and direct challenge to the illegalities of noncompetitive practice yet is wrapped in the mantle of judicial approbation.

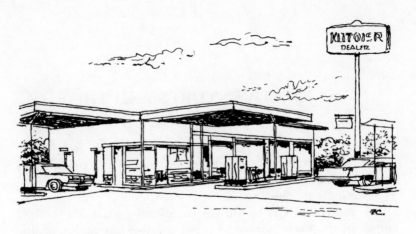

Types of Joint Ventures

Joint ventures may be classified according to different criteria. They may be horizontal, vertical and conglomerate. A horizontal illustration is the combination of two or more oil companies combining to do exploration. A vertical venture is the combination of a oil company and, for example, a chemical company in which each contributes to the process of manufacture or sale or both. A conglomerate venture is one in which the oil company may combine with a company in another industry, for example steel, in which the product of the joined firms is yet a third product, perhaps hotel building.

Joint ventures may be classified as domestic or foreign depending on the area in which they operate. This difference is significant because what may not be tolerated at home may in fact be encouraged abroad.

There are temporary and permanent joint ventures, that is, their longevity is governed by the duration of their existence. The venture may get together for a specific objective and having achieved that objective, then disband. Oil companies bidding on off-shore leases are an illustration of this combination. Then, of course, there is the permanent venture in which the new corporation continues in existence into the future. A pipeline venture suits this illustration.

The purpose of a joint venture is encased in goodness. It increases the ability to raise capital, to spread the risk, to make use of complementary or overlapping techniques or research and to achieve potential economies of vertical integration. Real technological progress may be made by pooling the energies and talents of diverse firms. They are advantageous to society when they result in lowering of costs (with a consequent reduction of price). Where partners to a joint bidding arrangement are not able to bid independently because of risk and capital requirements, then a combination not only does not eliminate bidders, it increases the number of bidding units by one. Again a joint venture which is formed by firms who would not have the needed capital to engage in the enterprise individually may provide additional competition in any given industrial situation.

From the point of view of economic power, the controlling motive in most if not all instances where joint ventures have been formed is the desire to increase the degree of integration of the parent companies. The one basic motive is the desire to avoid competition.

The Anti-Competitive Nature of Joint Ventures

The following illustrates how joint ventures may become anti-competitive and because they are widespread in the oil industry, how dangerous they can become.

Avoidance of competition: Community of interest and need for a harmonious relationship among parents for the successful management of their offspring may lead to preferred treatment in the vertical market relationship among the parents. Avoidance is sometimes actual and sometimes potential. Wherever there is a greater degree of vertical integration, competition is abridged. The inevitable result of such an intercorporate relationship is the elimination of potential or actual competition.

Where the joint venture is in a horizontal relationship to the parent firms, important dimensions of competition such as ·price and non-price competition, as well as levels of output and geogra-

---

[9] Stanley E. Boyle, "The Joint Subsidiary: An Economic Appraisal," The Antitrust Bulletin, May-June 1960.

phical markets to be served, must be decided upon. Cooperation is in fact a prerequisite to success of the joint venture.

Given the profit incentive which guides firm behavior, neither of the parent firms will behave like a competitor with respect to its offspring since it would be competing with its own profit share. The incentive to cooperate instead, is of the same character as that between a firm and one of its own divisions or subsidiaries. The strength of the incentive is weakened only by the less than 100% ownership and consequent percentage claim on profits.

Price is also affected. In petroleum mining, for example, if there is a profitable market for petroleum, then each partner will attempt to increase production of crude petroleum. If on the other hand the market is unfavorable, each partner will insist that the other buy his full quota or all agree that output should be reduced. Thus, a vertical relationship may contribute further to final product output policy among parents.

A common meeting place: The joint venture allows a common meeting place in which the supposedly competitive firms may legally meet. It makes the development of common patterns of action a simple matter because they have "legitimate" reasons for consulting with one another. It is inconceivable that firms engaged cooperatively in one industrial area would not act the same way in others. There obviously exists the possibility that the partners themselves would be less likely to compete with each other because of their joint undertaking. The marriage introduces the possibility of harmony rather than competition between the parents. As a practical matter, there is no way of divorcing the management of the joint subsidiary from friendliness between the parents.

Concentration of economic power: A joint venture has behind it the economic power of not just one but two or more companies. Therefore it allows firms to pool their financial resources and the resulting venture obtains an advantage over other firms in the industry. When the involved firms are giants in their respective areas, it undoubtedly leads to a greater concentration of economic power.

Joint ventures have little justification if the financial resources of one or both of the companies are sufficient to undertake the enterprise singly. Recognizing the enormous size of the joint ventures in the oil industry, it is hard to appreciate the share-the-risk

44

concept against the social losses that could accrue to society from anti-competitive behavior.

Exchange of information and production planning: Co-venturers must work together in developing plans within the "joint area of interest." Each becomes familiar with the others' areas of special interest and even with their methods of evaluation. Information must be exchanged on changing interest. This process of "learning to live with each other" is an essential characteristic of joint ventures. Men in a close working relationship would be expected to consider each others' interest and behavioral patterns.

Most American oil companies are associated through a multitude of joint ventures in petroleum exploration and mining. Thus, in these cases the joint venture supplies raw materials to the parents who compete in various segments of oil refining and distribution. Where the joint venture supplies the crude petroleum to two or more parent firms, then the situation may require a close degree of cooperation between the parents. This follows from the fact that the parents have a claim on a certain physical volume of their joint venture's output, and the partners output is a function of their joint venture's output.

It also implies a close check on the co-venturers' plans for expansion. There is an implied pledge not to expand output faster than the group interest would approve. In the Aramco joint venture, nominations are 1 year firm and 3 years tentative; each member not only has a precise idea of his partners' short run plans, but at least a good idea of their long run plans for permanent expansion. If output were increased, it might have to build refineries and distribution terminals in other countries which would be another source of information to the joint venture. Thus, each party is aware of the plans of all the other parties.

Compounding the effect of information exchange and production planning is the overlapping membership in joint ventures. If the production plans of Gulf Oil are known to its partner, British Petroleum (Kuwait Oil Company), they must also be known to British Petroleum's five partners in the Iraq Petroleum Company (Shell, CFP, Exxon, Mobil and the Gulbenkian interest). Standard of California and Texaco also share ventures with one or the other. As a result, each of the Persian Gulf producing companies takes account of the action of all others. Thus even if the companies do not confer on their production plans, each can be assured that nothing is contemplated to threaten an excess of supply and a threat to the price. Each can hold back on output in the almost certain knowledge that all others are doing the same.[10]

Joint bidding: This combination method is common in the oil industry and has been justified on the basis of the great risk involved. In any given sale it is obvious that when four firms, each able to bid independently, combine to submit a single bid, three interested potential bidders have been eliminated, that is, the combination has restrained trade. This situation does not differ materially from one of explicit collusion in which four firms meet in advance of a given sale and decide who among them should bid (which three should refrain from bidding) for specific leases and, instead of competing among themselves, attempt to rotate the winning bids.

It can be shown that within any given sale and geographical market, that is Alaska or the Gulf, when firms are partners in a joint bidding venture they very rarely bid against each other for other tracts offered as part of the same sale. In Alaska, where 885 bids were examined, only 16 cases were found where 2 partner firms had submitted opposing bids for any tract included in the same sale in which they participated as joint bidders. As one should expect, simultaneous joint bidding and competitive bidding is a rare event.

The record in the Gulf, further confirms that joint bidding partners do not bid against each other with the same frequency that they bid against non-partners although the propensity to avoid competition diminishes over a longer time period.

If joint bidding and subsequent bidding restraint among former partners reduces the number of bidders contending for specific tracts, it may involve serious pricing consequences. It can be shown that the high bid is a positive function of the number of bidders.

Despite carefully prepared analyses showing the impact of joint ventures on bidding practices to a meaningful level of significance, extensive interviews with oil company officers generate almost universal denial that a joint bidding agreement could lead to subsequent cooperation or restrained bidding.[11]

---

[10] Adelman, "The World Petroleum Market," Resources for the Future, 1973.

[11] For a more complete discussion of joint bidding, see Walter J. Mead, "The Competitive Significance of Joint Ventures," The Antitrust Bulletin, Fall 1967.

Foreclosure: One result of a joint venture is the elimination of part of the market of those who would supply the raw material to the fabricating firms and a reduction in the number of alternatives available to those who might be interested in purchasing the raw material. This is the concept of foreclosure.

Also of competitive significance is the issuance of potential competition where foreclosure results among members of the joint venture as well as to outside competitors. When two or more firms engage in a joint venture to establish a new entity, there is a net gain of one semi-independent firm in the industry entered, but perhaps at the expense of precluding entry by one or more of the parents separately. Further, potential competition due to future expansion into products and markets served by a partner may be precluded out of an interest to preserve a harmonious parental relationship.

Joint ventures behave like mergers: Many of the adverse results which may be expected through the outright merger of two or more companies may be obtained through a joint venture. Mergers frequently create an unnecessary agglomeration of wealth, reduce competition, and result in higher prices. It is indeed ironic when the Department of Justice or the various courts vigorously opposed the merger of two parents who then assume to themselves a green light to form a joint venture which has the status of a quasi-merger and obtains many of the objectionable results of outright merger.

Judicial or legislative sanction: When the Congress and the Department of Justice approved joint ventures, they in effect approved the venture but not the actions which might flow from that venture. Legal sanction, however, tends to introduce a structural impediment to the effective consummation of antitrust policy. After approving the establishment of the joint ventures, how strongly could the Department of Justice ask for diverstiture? And if such a request were received by the courts would they be willing or consider themselves able to honor it considering that the Department of Justice and Congress approved the establishment of the joint venture? Probably not in either instance.

Widespread Nature of Joint Ventures in the Oil Industry

The nature of joint ventures, as revealed above, lends considerable support to the hypothesis that they are incompatible with arms-length competition. Now let us turn to the joint venture as an instrument of operation in the oil industry.

What becomes immediately apparent is a staggering number of company inter-relationships which stretch around the world. In examining the many hundreds of such relationships among the major oil companies, the conclusion is clear that the joint venture is a dearly beloved form of mutual cooperation among them.

It should be clear at the outset that this study, in presenting listings and tabular data on joint ventures, makes no pretense at having a complete file of such combinations. That was manifestly impossible. In fact, we have no estimate even of the proportion which our listing of 154 ventures represents of the total number in the oil industry although their assets as a percent of the total is probably much higher than their relative numbers. We can, however, allude to information gaps, the closing of which requires resources far beyond the capacities of this effort.[12]

---

[12] The Central Intelligence Agency apparently thinks oil joint ventures important enough to allocate resources to compile such a list. Nevertheless, the Department of the Interior which informed us of its existence, claims it is a secret or confidential document and not for public release.

Already mentioned are the literally thousands of joint bidding arrangements, many of which acquire permanent status when oil and gas have been discovered.

There are joint ventures in which oil and gas companies share terminal facilities. Another coming to our attention is a microwave system shared by Atlantic-Richfield and Union Oil. Still another is a products station involving Texaco, Union Oil and Gulf.

Obtaining data on the number of joint ventures is a major difficulty in that corporate balance sheets may list them as a part of total investment. Also, many of them escape notice because the SEC only requires the listing of the joint venture in which a firm owns at least 50% of the stock. Thus in cases where three or more companies holding equal ownership exist, the listing of such ownership is not required and therefore most likely unreported. This factor alone would render the development of adequate data on the number and importance of joint ventures a herculean or impossible task. One estimate of the incidence of joint ventures suggests that there are some 345 of them owned by the 1,000 largest manufacturing companies in the United States.[13] We have uncovered 154 joint ventures, worldwide, among the largest American oil firms (see Appendix I).

Lurking behind all of the formalized ventures are those which are not formalized but have all the perquisites of joint and binding relationships. Included among them are the exchange agreements or supply partnerships in which Company X, for example, agrees to refine gallonage for Company Y in its refinery if the latter will do likewise for it at Y's refinery. Reduction in transportation costs accrues to the advantage of the partners.[14]

Nevertheless, the joint ventures shown in the report are more than ample to illustrate the concept of working agreements which the major oil companies have with one another. The categories of information gathered are as follows:

1. Oil company (only) joint ventures around the world.—We divided the world into six geographic areas: Asia and Australia, Europe, Africa, the Middle East, South America, and North Amer-

---

[13] Stanley Boyle "The Joint Subsidiary: An Economic Appraisal."

[14] The Federal Trade Commission, among others, is aware of these practices. Whether they are doing something about them is unclear since inquiries have failed to elict response.

ica (exclusive of U.S. joint venture pipelines). Each area has a separate tabulation and there is also a tabulation of all six worldwide regions combined.

2. Oil industry ventures with other industries.—The relationships contain a variety of combinations. There is one in which an oil company (Kerr-McGee) and a chemical company (American Cyanamid) combined to mine and process phosphate rock. There is another in which an oil company (Gulf) combines with airline company (Pan American) to build and operate European motels (if there is a gas station on the premises, what might be the brand?). Again, there were many combinations of an oil company with other companies to mine and process nuclear materials. Obtaining a list of ventures for this category was most difficult and the 18 shown is undoubtedly a fraction of those in existence.

3. Joint ventures in the pipeline industry in the United States. —Joint venture U.S. pipelines represent one of the oil industry's most frequent types of combinations. Although there are actually 29 U.S. joint venture pipelines, all listed in the appendix, our analysis

of interlocking partners as shown in our tables and charts is confined to only those with the largest operating revenues.

Pipeline systems, of which there are 21 listed in the appendix are shown separately because their corporate structures and operations are different from joint venture pipelines and in practice tend to be separated from the joint venture systems.

The oil pipeline joint venture is a structurally independent corporate offspring of two or more parents. It has its own officers and directors and maintains a set of accounting books relating to its total activities. The oil pipeline system, in accounting terms, is not an identifiable venture. Although the physical properties have identical characteristics to the joint venture, that is, there are miles of pipeline jointly owned, each partner's share is merged with the figures for the parent company and the system does not appear as a separate corporate entity. Although systems are regulated by the ICC, there are no statistics on them inasmuch as their operations are concealed in the parent company's total operation.

Choice of a "system" type of structure over the joint venture may reflect a tax situation because the parent has greater flexibility in allocating the profit within the total organization rather than to an identifiable venture corporation. Also, some financing advantages may accrue to individual partners in the "system" setup.

4. Joint bidding in the oil industry.—Joint bidding differs from joint ventures with respect to a time constraint. Two or more oil companies combine on a joint bid which, if successful, may result in an end to the working relationship. On the other hand, if the bid is successful the relationship may continue for an indeterminate period of time as a joint venture. Sometimes bidding arrangements are formed which continue from one bidding circumstance to another and the combination stays active even though individual bids may not be successful.

Bids in North America involving largely three areas—the Gulf of Mexico, Alaska, and the California Coast—have taken place over many years and the information on these bids is extremely voluminous. In Alaska, one study covered 885 bids in that State alone. Strangely enough, while there is precise information on individual bidding circumstances in each of the North American areas, we have been unable to locate official analyses of them.

THE FINDINGS

U.S. Oil Pipeline Ventures

Joint ventures in the oil pipeline industry appear to be one of the most popular expressions of oil industry commingling in the United States. An extraordinary network of company inter-relationships has evolved in the Nation's pipeline joint ventures. These pipelines in 1971 accounted for 25% of the Nation's total operating revenues of interstate oil pipelines but only 17% of the mileage (Table 11).

Reference to Chart IV and Table 12 reveals the nature and frequency of these relationships. Among the 16 largest oil pipeline ventures, Texaco is involved in 8 different ones; fifteen of the largest oil companies in the land are involved in the same 8 ventures with Texaco. But these numbers tell only part of the story. In fact, Texaco is involved with Mobil Oil and Cities Service no fewer than five times each in separate pipeline ventures and has four working relationships with Shell Oil in four ventures. In total, for domestic oil pipelines only, Texaco has no fewer than 38 working relationships with major oil companies in this country. Texaco representatives have the opportunity to present their point of view with respect to the venture, and perhaps inadvertently to discuss other matters of consequence with their partners for a total of 38 exposures (five with Mobil, five with Cities Service, four with Shell, etc.). But even that number is a vast understatement. The 38 exposures reflect only one meeting per year per joint venture. If the partners in each joint venture were to meet once a month, 12 times a year, their Texaco representatives would be exposed to individual partners a total of 456 times (38 x 12).

Sheer size of oil company is not necessarily related to the frequency of contact. Union Oil and Cities Service, for example, the 14th and 16th largest oil companies, had no fewer than 32 working relationships each with their other cooperative oil companies. Continental Oil, 10th largest company, had the second largest number of confrontations. Even lilliputian (?) Clark Oil, 28th largest firm, enjoyed 15 relationships. Multiply these numbers by a reasonable 12 meetings a year and the dulcet conversational exchanges in combination could rise to several octaves above a thunderous clap.

Apart from the problem of economic justification of joint own-

Table 11. Joint Venture Oil Pipelines, U.S. Mileage, Barrels, Assets and Operating Revenues January 1, 1972

Jt. Venture Pipeline [1]	Mileage	Barrels received into system (add 000's)	Total Assets (add 000's)	Operating Revenues (add 000's)
Arapahoe	1,501	25,446	13,423	4,289
Badger	331	44,471	12,361	4,592
Black Lake	255	10,765	9,240	1,575
Butte	511	26,185	11,096	4,128
Cherokee	2,377	72,010	13,638	7,263
Chicap	234	51,700	25,589	2,516
Colonial	3,690	426,782	480,195	108,819
Cook Inlet	55	52,210	39,063	11,807
Four Corners	909	13,147	20,940	5,548
Jayhawk	695	30,178	14,383	3,350
Kaw	1,433	21,965	5,388	2,190
Lake Charles	12	69,693	3,844	988
Laurel	451	41,692	35,856	7,009
Mid-Valley	1,004	116,504	37,648	15,909
Olympic	314	48,682	30,687	7,218
Pioneer	303	6,454	5,042	1,923
Plantation	3,948	171,079	176,089	46,584
Platte	1,257	56,049	33,019	11,727
Portal	761	7,401	20,800	3,127
Southcap [2]	—	35,466	28,672	5,674
Tecumseh	206	29,539	9,088	1,556
Texaco-C. Service	2,155	103,270	17,059	6,923
Texas-N. Mexico	5,121	162,116	30,515	13,706
West Shore	296	53,991	17,561	6,286
West Texas Gulf	581	132,871	19,756	8,423
White Shoal [2]	8	9,284	2,730	815
Wolverine	455	40,716	21,817	4,962
Wyco	731	18,741	14,073	5,072
Yellowstone	751	18,246	15,992	6,480
Jt. venture total [3]	30,345	1,896,653	1,165,564	310,459
U.S. pipeline total	174,722	8,341,531	4,951,400	1,249,298
Jt. ventures, %	17.4	22.7	23.5	24.9

[1] For identity of co-venturers, see appendix I.

[2] Excludes mileage represented by respondent's undivided interest in system(s) operated by another carrier or other carriers.

[3] Explorer Pipeline, a large facility, began operation in December 1971, and hence not shown in compilation.

Source: Pipeline Statistics from Transport Statistics in the United States, December 31, 1971, Part 6, Pipelines, Interstate Commerce Commission. Identification of joint ventures from ICC's ACV reports.

Table 12. United States Pipeline Joint Ventures[1]

	St. Oil (N.J.)	Mobil Oil	Texaco	Gulf Oil	BP	St. Oil (Cal.)	St. Oil (Ind.)	Shell Oil	Atlantic Rich.	Continental	Phillips	Union Oil	Sun Oil	Cities Service	St. Oil (Ohio)	Getty Oil	Marathon	Clark Oil	Joint Ventures Involved In	Companies Involved In	Working Relationships
St. Oil (N.J.)		1	1			1	1	2		2		2		1			2	1	3	10	14
Mobil Oil	1		5	1	1		3	2	1	2	1	3		2			2	2	5	13	26
Texaco	1	5		3	2		3	4	2	3	2	2	1	5	2	1	2	2	8	15	38
Gulf Oil		1	3		2	1	1	2	3	5	2	3	3	2			1		8	14	31
BP		1	2	2			1		1	1	1	1		1					3	9	11
St. Oil (Cal.)	1			1			2	2	1	1									2	5	6
St. Oil (Ind.)	1	3	3	1	1	2		1	1	2	1	2	1	1			1	1	3	13	19
Shell Oil	2	2	4	2		2	1		1	3	1	2	1	3			2	2	6	14	28
Atlantic Rich.		1	2	3	1	1	1	1		3	1	2		2		1	2		4	13	20
Continental	2	2	3	5	1	1	2	3	3		2	4	1	2			2	1	7	15	34
Phillips		1	2	2	1		1	1	1	2		1	1	2					2	11	15

Table 12. United States Pipeline Joint Ventures (Cont'd)

	St. Oil (N.J.)	Mobil Oil	Texaco	Gulf Oil	BP	St. Oil (Cal.)	St. Oil (Ind.)	Shell Oil	Atlantic Rich.	Continental	Phillips	Union Oil	Sun Oil	Cities Service	St. Oil (Ohio)	Getty Oil	Marathon	Clark Oil	Joint Ventures Involved In	Companies Involved In	Working Relationships
Union Oil	2	3	2	3	1		2	2	2	4	1		1	3	1		3	2	6	15	32
Sun Oil	1		1	3				1		1	1	1		2	2				3	8	12
Cities Service		2	5	2	1		1	3	2	2	2	1			1		2	2	7	16	32
St. Oil (Ohio)				2							2	3	2	1		1			2	4	6
Getty Oil			1						1			1	2	1					1	3	3
Marathon	2	2	2	1			1	2	1	2		3		2				2	3	11	20
Clark Oil	1	2	2				1	2		1		2		2			2		2	9	15
Total																			75		362

[1] This table is based on data which include only the 16 largest pipeline joint ventures in the U.S., based on operating revenue, 1971.

55

Chart IV. Participating Members*
Ten Largest Joint Venture Pipelines in the U.S., 1972

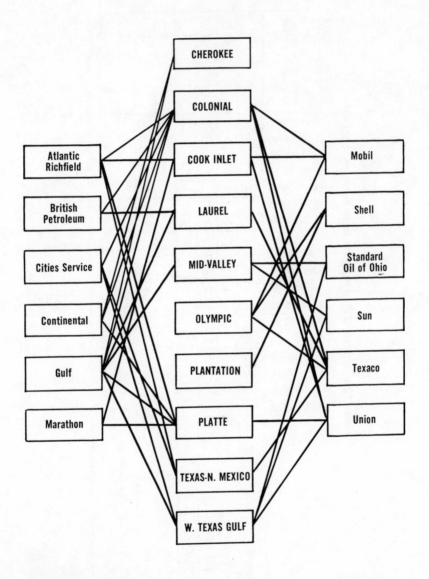

* Chart shows only those oil companies in 2 or more of the joint venture pipelines listed
above. Standard of Indiana and Phillips Petroleum are co-venturers in Colonial; Exxon
and SoCal are members of Plantation; and Getty participates in Texas-N. Mexico.
56

ership of pipelines, the frequency of inter-company exposure and participation unquestionably provides opportunities for exchange of information, a discussion of marketing priorities, perhaps some production planning, and perhaps a general forum in which a climate of unanimity with respect to such problems as scarcity, prices, political associations and other pertinent affairs can be developed.

U.S. Pipeline "Systems"

Ten pipeline systems have been identified in Chart V. Apart from the difference in corporate structure distinguishing the "system" from the joint venture, the opportunities for mutual discussions appear to be the same.

The system concept appears to be most appealing to Atlantic Richfield which has no fewer than six such participations. Conspicuous by its absence is Continental Oil for which we have been unable to find any system membership under its own name. It will be recalled that Continental participated in at least seven pipeline joint ventures.

The gas pipeline industry is remarkably free of joint agreements. With the exception of the Great Lakes Transmission venture, owned half and half by American Natural Gas and a Canadian Company, and the Sea Robin Pipeline Company, owned jointly by United Gas Pipeline and Southern Natural Gas Company, there are at present no operating joint ventures in this very sizable industry. The circumstance may have its origin in the unique development of natural gas usage. In the early stages of gas development, the oil companies considered natural gas a waste product and were more than eager to dispose of it to whomever would take it off their hands. This policy opened the field for natural gas to companies outside the petroleum industry. The former raised their smaller capital requirements on an individual basis and subsequently became large enough to maintain the individual proprietorship of these enterprises.

Oil Industry Joint Ventures Abroad

The frequency of contact between oil companies in the United States through their pipeline joint ventures has been amply demon-

Chart V. Participating Members*
Ten Largest Pipeline "Systems" in the U.S., 1972

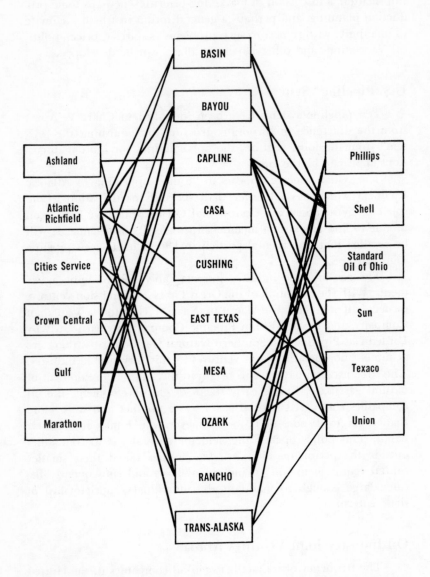

* Chart shows only those oil companies in 2 or more of the pipeline "systems" listed above. Standard of Indiana and Clark are co-venturers in Capline; Amerada Hess, BP, Exxon, and Mobil are members of Trans-Alaska.

strated. It now remains to be seen how frequently the oil companies via their joint ventures are involved on an international basis. For it seems obvious that if there are opportunities for multiple conversations and relationships in the United States as well as elsewhere around the world, then the picture of intercompany action would be complete.

It is necessary to distinguish between involvements at home and abroad. In view of the prospective shortage of oil and gas in the United States, the State Department as a political policy may have encouraged the oil companies to act in concert in a manner which it probably would not sanction here at home. On the other hand, these joint relationships, particularly in the Persian Gulf, have been a part of oil company operations reaching back several decades when these companies had a relatively free hand and used their inter-relationships as a normal way of doing business.

The extent to which oil companies should be permitted to operate in a joint manner, say as between the U.S. and the Persian Gulf or with respect to Japan, Europe and South America is a distinction which the government through the President, the State Department, or the Congress should decide. The purpose here is to show the web of entanglements that exists among major oil companies around the world, and how it is possible, perhaps necessary, to discuss oil developments in every sector of the world, including the impact on world and domestic prices and industry policy.

The stage for joint action around the world is well designed. We have isolated no fewer than 75 international joint ventures (although with a marked feeling of inadequacy as respects the total number). Europe leads the array with 24 joint ventures followed by between 11 and 15 each in other parts of the world (table 13). In North America, if one adds both the U.S. selected pipeline joint ventures as well as other ventures in Alaska and Canada, the number is expanded to well over 100.[15] Companies participating in more than 30 ventures worldwide include Exxon, Mobil, Texaco, BP and Shell. Individual company participations are not additive since two or more of them may be involved in the same joint venture.

Again, it is the number of working relationships that provide

---

[15] The number of ventures listed in the appendix exceed those in the tables. That is because new ventures came to our attention after the tabulations were completed.

Table 13. Selected Oil Industry Joint Ventures by Area of the World, 1972

Size Rank	Company	Africa	Asia & Australia	Europe	Middle East	South America	North America	U.S. Pipeline	Total[1]
1	Exxon	1	4	10	8	2	3	3	31
2	Mobil	2	7	5	9	2	2	5	32
3	Texaco	2	3	7	6	9	3	8	38
4	Gulf Oil	1	0	1	4	2	3	8	19
5	BP	7	6	12	8	1	1	3	38
6	St. Oil (Cal.)	1	3	4	5	1	2	2	18
7	St. Oil (Ind)	0	0	1	0	1	3	3	8
8	Shell Oil	9	5	15	4	6	2	6	47
9	Atlantic R.	0	0	0	3	3	3	4	13
10	Continental	2	0	3	2	0	0	7	14
11	Tenneco	0	0	0	0	0	1	0	1
12	Occidental	0	0	0	0	0	1	0	1
13	Phillips	0	0	0	1	1	2	2	5
14	Union Oil	0	0	0	0	0	1	6	9
15	Sun Oil	1	0	0	2	3	1	3	10
16	Cities Service	0	0	0	1	1	2	7	11
17	Ashland Oil	0	0	0	0	0	1	0	1
18	St. Oil (Ohio)	0	0	1	1	0	2	2	5
19	Amerada Hess	1	0	1	0	0	0	0	2
20	Getty Oil	0	1	0	1	0	0	1	3
21	Signal	0	0	0	0	0	1	0	1
22	Marathon	1	0	3	0	0	2	3	9
23	Kerr McGee	1	0	0	1	0	0	0	1
27	Am. Petrofina	1	0	1	0	0	0	0	2
28	Clark Oil	1	0	0	0	0	0	2	3
29	Commonwealth	0	0	0	0	1	0	0	1
	Total Ventures	11	12	24	15	13	9	16	100[1]

[1] Totals for companies are not additive since two or more may be involved in the same joint venture.

the significant clue to inter-company collaboration. The 100 selected joint ventures require that representatives of oil companies have a minimum of 1062 confrontations (assuming there is one meeting per year per venture) to discuss plans and problems (Table 14). In business enterprises of that magnitude it is not unreasonable for meetings for a single venture to take place more than once a year. Therefore the figure on inter-company confrontations of 1062 needs to be multiplied by the number of times each venture meets. If they met once a month, the number of confrontations would exceed 12,000 annually, twice a month, 24,000, etc.

In this wide melange of inter-company discussions concerning operations in single parts of the world, can there be any doubt that there must be a central force with respect to each company that pulls the pieces together? In the complex world of oil production, transmission, refining and marketing, is it possible for one venture in one part of the world to operate as an independent entity without regard to the other pieces of this worldwide jigsaw puzzle?

We leave it to the imagination of the most humble business man—perhaps the 220,000 service station operators whom Mobil considers its competitors but who wait vainly for the telephone call that summons them to these lofty worldwide meetings—to make a judgment of the frequency of flow of information from these thousands of meetings around the world back home to the central office of the oil company involved. Indeed, also to imagine the reverse flow of instructions which emanate from the central office to its employees around the world on how to behave in a marketing or price situation within their limited business domain. He should have little difficulty in imagining the participants in the joint venture, each supplied with multiple instructions from the home office, discussing the various pros and cons of both the local and international oil markets as a backdrop for making decisions with respect to the task immediately at hand. Then, if we may borrow some terminology from the computer world, these same outposts like terminals, flash the information back to the main frame for analysis and policy making.

While there may not be any overt attempt at collaboration in a conspiratorial sense, the common interest of the joint venture participants plus the exchange of information on a local and world basis certainly provide the opportunity for anti-competitive action

Table 14. Selected Oil Industry Joint Venture Working Relationships,[1] by Area of the World, 1972

Size Rank	Company	Africa	Asia & Australia	Europe	Middle East	South America	North America	U.S. Pipeline	Total[1]
1	Exxon	1	10	22	29	3	14	14	93
2	Mobil Oil	8	11	13	31	2	6	26	97
3	Texaco	8	8	18	25	16	12	38	125
4	Gulf Oil	1	0	1	13	2	17	31	65
5	BP	13	6	24	24	1	1	11	80
6	St. Oil (Cal.)	4	6	7	21	1	8	6	53
7	St. Oil (Ind.)	0	0	1	0	2	12	19	34
8	Shell Oil	17	10	26	17	11	11	28	120
9	Atlantic R.	0	0	0	14	6	13	20	53
10	Continental	4	0	8	13	0	0	34	59
11	Tenneco	0	0	0	0	0	7	0	7
12	Occidental	0	0	0	0	0	7	0	7
13	Phillips	0	0	0	0	3	9	15	27
14	Union Oil	0	0	0	1	0	11	32	44
15	Sun Oil	1	0	0	6	7	1	12	27
16	Cities Service	0	0	0	3	2	10	32	47
17	Ashland Oil	0	0	0	0	0	7	0	7
18	St. Oil (Ohio)	0	0	0	10	0	3	6	19
19	Amerada Hess	3	0	1	0	0	0	0	4
20	Getty Oil	0	5	0	10	0	0	3	18
21	Signal	0	0	0	0	0	7	0	7
22	Marathon	3	0	10	0	0	8	20	41
23	Kerr McGee	0	0	0	3	0	0	0	3
24	Am. Petrofina	4	0	3	0	0	0	0	7
25	Clark Oil	1	0	0	0	0	0	15	16
26	Commonwealth	0	0	0	0	2	0	0	2
	Total	68	56	134	220	58	164	362	1062

[1] Defined as individual or group discussions with joint venture partners on a once-a-year meeting basis. Multiply number by frequency of meetings per year.

on a global scale. Tables 15 through 21 show this extraordinary worldwide web for a selected 100 ventures.

Joint venture arrangements would seem to simplify more sophisticated attempts at proving collusion by other means. Why one needs to go through devious pathways of secondary interlocks and tertiary control mechanisms to prove possible collusion when oil companies nurture their joint relationships for all the world to see is a judicial and legislative conundrum.

Oil Company Penetration Into Other Industries Via the Joint Venture

Judging by the frequency with which oil companies have gone outside their own industry to form joint ventures, one may assume that this form of corporate endeavor is almost as popular as outright acquisition.

In hearings before a Senate antitrust committee, it was revealed that 20 large petroleum companies between 1956 and 1968 acquired 95 companies outside the industry for an average of eight per year.[16]

An examination of admittedly incomplete newspaper files of the Federal Trade Commission shows that in the five-year period of 1967-71, 19 joint venture agreements were established by 11 oil companies in other industries or an average of four per year (Table 22).

The most popular joint venture activity was reflected in combinations with six nuclear energy companies. In two other instances, however, Gulf and Continental combined with Allied Chemical and Aerojet General respectively to process nuclear fuel.

Occidental combined with Holiday Inns to construct motels and, while apparently successful in Europe, was at loggerheads with the Moroccan Government. Gulf and Pan Am also joined to build and operate motels in Europe.

Shell joined with the Union Pacific R.R. to explore for oil while Eastern Gas and Fuel Associates combined with the same railroad to mine low-sulphur coal. (For complete list of participants, see appendix.)

---

[16] "Governmental Intervention in the Market Mechanism," Hearings before the Subcommittee on Antitrust and Monopoly, 91st Congress, The Petroleum Industry, Part 3, July 1969, p. 1179.

Table 15. Joint Venture Summary (100 Ventures)

	St. Oil (N.J.)	Mobil Oil	Texaco	Gulf Oil	BP	St. Oil (Cal.)	St. Oil (Ind.)	Shell Oil	Atlantic Rich.	Continental	Tenneco	Occidental	Phillips	Union Oil	Sun Oil	Cities Service	Ashland Oil	St. Oil (Ohio)	Amerada Hess	Getty Oil	Signal	Marathon	Kerr-McGee	Am. Petrofina	Clark Oil	Commonwealth	Joint Ventures Involved In	Companies Involved With	Working Relationships
St. Oil (N.J.)		15	15	4	9	8	2	17	2	4	1	1		3		2	2	1		2		4		1	1		31	19	93
Mobil Oil	15		18	2	12	8	4	15	2	4			3	4		2		2		2		3			2		32	17	97
Texaco	15	18		7		12	4	18	5	7	1		3	3	5	5		1		3		3		1	2	1	38	22	125
Gulf Oil	4	2	7		6	3	3	5	6	6				4	3	4	1	3	1	1	1	2					19	20	65
BP	9	12		6				23	2	4				1	1	1	1	2	1	1		2		2			38	17	80
St. Oil (Cal.)	8	8	12	3				6		2				1	1	1	1	1	1	2	1	1					18	15	53
St. Oil (Ind.)	2	4	4	3				2	4	2	1		2	2	2	2	1	1	1	2	1	1			1		8	18	34
Shell Oil	17	15	18	5	23	6	2		4	7				3	3	3		1	1	2	1	4			2		47	23	120
Atlantic Rich.	2	2	5	6	2		4	4				4		4	2	6		1	1	2	1	2	2				13	18	53
Continental	4	4	7	6	4	2	2	7						2	2	2		1	1	1	1	5		1			14	18	59
Tenneco	1		1				1					1					1	1									1	7	7
Occidental	1										1						1										1	7	7
Phillips		3	3				2		4					2	2	3					1	1		1	2		5	14	27

64

Table 15. Joint Venture Summary (100 Ventures) (Cont'd)

	St. Oil (N.J.)	Mobil Oil	Texaco	Gulf Oil	BP	St. Oil (Cal.)	St. Oil (Ind.)	Shell Oil	Atlantic Rich.	Continental	Tenneco	Occidental	Phillips	Union Oil	Sun Oil	Cities Service	Ashland Oil	St. Oil (Ohio)	Amerada Hess	Getty Oil	Signal	Marathon	Kerr-McGee	Am. Petrofina	Clark Oil	Commonwealth	Joint Ventures Involved In	Companies Involved With	Working Relationships
Union Oil	3	4	3	4	1	1	2	3	4	4			2		1	4		1			1	4			2		9	17	44
Sun Oil			5	3	1			2	3	2			2	1		3		2				1	1		1		10	13	27
Cities Service	2	2	5	4	1	1	2	3	6	2			3	4	3			1		1	1	3	1		2		11	19	47
Ashland Oil	1		1	1			1	1	1													1					1	7	7
St. Oil (Ohio)	1		1	3	2	1	1	2	1	1	1	1		1	2	1											5	14	19
Amerada Hess								1	1	1										1							2	4	4
Getty Oil			1	2	2	1	1	3	2	2			2			1			1								3	11	18
Signal								1	1	1			1	1		1						1					1	7	7
Marathon	4	3	3	2	2	1	1	4	2	5			1	4	1	3	1				1		1		2		9	18	41
Kerr-McGee															1	1						1					1	3	3
Am. Petrofina		1	1	1				1	1																2		2	6	7
Clark Oil		2	1				1	2		1				2	1	2						2		2			3	10	16
Commonwealth			1					1																			1	2	2
																											323	346	1,062

65

Table 16. Joint Ventures In The Middle East

	St. Oil (N.J.)	Mobil Oil	Texaco	Gulf Oil	BP	St. Oil (Cal.)	Shell Oil	Atlantic Rich.	Continental	Union Oil	Sun Oil	Cities Service	St. Oil (Ohio)	Getty Oil	Kerr-McGee	Joint Ventures Involved In	Companies Involved With	Working Relationships
St. Oil (N.J.)		8	5	1	3	5	3	1	1				1	1		8	10	29
Mobil Oil	8		5	1	4	5	4	1	1				1	1		9	10	31
Texaco	5	5		1	2	5	1	1	2		1		1	1		6	11	25
Gulf Oil	1	1	1		4	1	1	1	1				1	1		4	10	13
BP	3	4	2	4		1	4	1	2		1		1	1		8	11	24
St. Oil (Cal.)	5	5	5	1	1			1	1				1	1		5	9	21
Shell Oil	3	4	1	1	4			1	1				1	1		4	9	17
Atlantic Rich.	1	1	1	1	1	1	1		1	1	1	1	1	1	1	3	14	14
Continental	1	1	2	1	2	1	1	1			1		1	1		2	11	13
Union Oil								1								1	1	1
Sun Oil			1		1			1	1			1			1	2	6	6
Cities Service								1			1				1	1	3	3
St. Oil (Ohio)	1	1	1	1	1	1	1	1	1					1		1	10	10
Getty Oil	1	1	1	1	1	1	1	1	1				1			1	10	10
Kerr-McGee								1			1	1				1	3	3
																56	128	220

Table 17. Joint Ventures In Africa

	St. Oil (N.J.)	Mobil Oil	Texaco	Gulf Oil	BP	St. Oil (Cal.)	Shell Oil	Continental	Sun Oil	Amerada Hess	Marathon	Am. Petrofina	Clark Oil	Joint Ventures Involved In	Companies Involved With	Working Relationships
St. Oil (N.J.)				1										1	1	1
Mobil Oil			2		2	1	2					1		2	5	8
Texaco		2			2	1	2					1		2	5	8
Gulf Oil	1													1	1	1
BP		2	2			1	7					1		7	5	13
St. Oil (Cal.)		1	1		1		1							1	4	4
Shell Oil		2	2		7	1		2		1	1	1		9	8	17
Continental							2			1	1			2	3	4
Sun Oil													1	1	1	1
Amerada Hess							1	1			1			1	3	3
Marathon							1	1		1				1	3	3
Am. Petrofina		1	1		1		1							1	4	4
Clark Oil									1					1	1	1
														30	44	68

67

Table 18. Joint Ventures In South America

	St. Oil (N.J.)	Mobil Oil	Texaco	Gulf Oil	BP	St. Oil (Cal.)	St. Oil (Ind.)	Shell Oil	Atlantic Rich.	Phillips	Sun Oil	Cities Service	Commonwealth	Totals		
														Joint Ventures Involved In	Companies Involved With	Working Relationships
St. Oil (N.J.)			1					2						2	2	3
Mobil Oil			2											2	1	2
Texaco				2				4	2	1	3		1	9	8	16
Gulf Oil														2	1	2
BP								1						1	1	1
St. Oil (Cal.)									1					1	1	1
St. Oil (Ind.)										1	1			1	2	2
Shell Oil										1	1	1	1	6	7	11
Atlantic Rich.											2	1		3	4	6
Phillips														1	3	3
Sun Oil														3	4	7
Cities Service														1	2	2
Commonwealth														1	2	2
														33	38	57

68

Table 19. Joint Ventures In Europe

	St. Oil (N.J.)	Mobil Oil	Texaco	Gulf Oil	BP	St. Oil (Cal.)	St. Oil (Ind.)	Shell Oil	Continental	Amerada Hess	Marathon	Am. Petrofina	Totals		
													Joint Ventures Involved In	Companies Involved With	Working Relationships
St. Oil (N.J.)		1	4		6	1		6	1		2	1	10	8	22
Mobil Oil	1		2		2	1		5	1		1		5	7	13
Texaco	4	2			3	3		3	2		1		7	7	18
Gulf Oil								1					1	1	1
BP	6	2	3			1		8	1		2	1	12	8	24
St. Oil (Cal.)	1	1	3		1			1					4	5	7
St. Oil (Ind.)										1			1	1	1
Shell Oil	6	5	3	1	8	1			1		1		15	8	26
Continental	1	1	2		1			1			2		3	6	8
Amerada Hess							1						1	1	1
Marathon	2	1	1		2			1	2			1	3	7	10
Am. Petrofina	1				1						1		1	3	3
													63	62	134

Table 20. Joint Ventures in North America (Other than Pipelines)

	St. Oil (N.J.)	Mobil Oil	Texaco	Gulf Oil	BP	St. Oil (Cal.)	St. Oil (Ind.)	Shell Oil	Atlantic Rich.	Tenneco	Occidental	Phillips	Union Oil	Sun Oil	Cities Service	Ashland Oil	St. Oil (Ohio)	Signal	Marathon	Joint Ventures Involved In	Companies Involved With	Working Relationships
St. Oil (N.J.)		1	2	2		1	1	2	1	1	1		1		1	1				3	12	15
Mobil Oil	1		1				1	1					1				1			2	6	6
Texaco	2	1				1	1	2	1	1	1		1			1				3	10	12
Gulf Oil	2					1	1	1	2	1	1	1	1		2	1	1	1	1	3	14	17
BP																	1			1	1	1
St. Oil (Cal.)	1		1	1			1	1		1	1	1								2	8	8
St. Oil (Ind.)	1	1	1	1		1		1	2	1	1	1	1							3	11	12
Shell Oil	2	1	2	1		1	1			1	1		1							2	9	11
Atlantic Rich.	1		1	2			2				1	2	1					1	2	3	9	13
Tenneco	1		1	1		1	1	1				1								1	7	7
Occidental	1		1	1		1	1	1	1											1	7	7
Phillips				1		1	1		2	1			1					1	1	2	8	9
Union Oil	1	1	1	1			1	1	1			1			1			1	1	2	11	11

Table 20. Joint Ventures in North Africa (Other than Pipelines) (Cont'd)

	St. Oil (N.J.)	Mobil Oil	Texaco	Gulf Oil	BP	St. Oil (Cal.)	St. Oil (Ind.)	Shell Oil	Atlantic Rich.	Tenneco	Occidental	Phillips	Union Oil	Sun Oil	Cities Service	Ashland Oil	St. Oil (Ohio)	Signal	Marathon	Joint Ventures Involved In	Companies Involved With	Working Relationships
Sun Oil																			1	1	1	1
Cities Service	1			2			1	2				1	1					1	1	2	8	10
Ashland Oil	1		1	1			1	1		1	1									1	7	7
St. Oil (Ohio)		1			1		1													2	3	3
Signal				1		1			1			1	1		1				1	1	7	7
Marathon				1		1			1			1	1	1	1			1		2	8	8
																				37	147	165

71

Table 21. Joint Ventures in Asia and Australia

| | St. Oil (N.J.) | Mobil Oil | Texaco | BP | St. Oil (Cal.) | Shell Oil | Getty Oil | Totals | | |
								Joint Ventures Involved In	Companies Involved With	Working Relationships
St. Oil (N.J.)..		4	2		1	2	1	4	5	10
Mobil Oil.....	4		1	3	1	1	1	7	6	11
Texaco.......	2	1			2	2	1	3	5	8
BP...........		3				3		6	2	6
St. Oil (Cal.)..	1	1	2			1	1	3	5	6
Shell Oil......	2	1	2	3	1		1	5	6	10
Getty Oil......	1	1	1		1	1		1	5	5
								29	34	56

Table 22. Joint Ventures Between Oil Companies
and Other Industries, U.S., 1967-71

Company	Nuclear Energy	Con-glom-erates	Chem-ical	Hotel Chains	Rail-road	Air-lines	Steel	Banks
Gulf Oil....	2	—	1	—	—	1	—	1
Shell Oil...	—	—	—	—	1	—	—	—
Atlantic R..	1	—	—	—	—	—	—	—
Continental	1	2	—	—	—	—	—	—
Occidental.	—	—	—	1	—	—	—	—
Union Oil..	1	—	—	—	—	—	—	—
Marathon..	1	—	—	—	—	—	—	—
Kerr McGee...	—	—	2	—	—	—	—	—
Diamond Sham....	—	—	—	—	—	—	1	—
EG&F Assoc....	—	—	—	—	1	—	—	—
Common-wealth...	—	2	—	—	—	—	—	—

Source: FTC files, newspaper clippings.

Joint Bidding

In terms of numbers alone, joint bidding on off-shore oil and gas exploration rank as the most numerous type of joint venture by far. Between 1954 and 1972, there was a total of 6,285 bids for rights mainly in Texas, Louisiana and California.[17] By actual count, 52% of the 1972 bids were joint participations and applying this percentage to the total, we estimate that some 3,300 of the bids over the years were joint participations. The average number of bidders per joint bid, again on sampling basis, averaged 3.3 companies.

Studies have confirmed (see p. 00) that partners rarely bid against each other for tracts offered as part of the same sale. It was also shown that the high bid is positively related to the number of bidders. Instead of hundreds of instances, therefore, here is a field of activity which has occurred thousands of times in which bidding combinations have resulted in lower bids than might have obtained otherwise.

Possible Remedies

The approach to joint ventures as a collusive practice is difficult because of the tolerant attitude taken by the courts and the Congress, and the less-than-effusive action of the Department of Justice.[18] Nevertheless, there are a number of directions which may be taken, some of which are stated below:

1. Every horizontal joint venture where the combined parental market share accounts for a certain proportion (20% or more has been suggested) in the relevant geographical market should be considered prima facie illegal. While no single oil company controls that percentage of the market nationwide, it has been stated [19] that in 1969 the 8 largest oil companies supplied about 54% of the na-

---

[17] U.S. Department of Interior, Bureau of Land Management, New Orleans, La.

[18] The Department "has initiated several investigations of joint venture petroleum pipelines, including the proposed TransAlaska Pipeline System." Letter of March 1, 1972, from Walker B. Comegys, Acting Assistant Attorney General Antitrust Division to Congressman Neal Smith, Chairman Subcommittee on Special Small Business Problems.

[19] Carl Kaysen and Donald Truner, "Antitrust Policy: An Economic and Legal Analysis."

tionwide oil market while their regional market penetration varied from 48% to 99%. Thus, joint venture parents who might not meet the market share limitation on a national basis may fall within its scope under a geographical-segmentation-of-the-market approach.

2. Where joint ventures involve vertically integrated parents, on the argument that close parental cooperation may yield the same anti-competitive results as a merger, a joint venture should be considered prima facie illegal where one parent firm has more than 20% of an industry's output in any relevant market and its partner has more than 5 to 10 percent of its industry's output.

3. It is suggested that the joint subsidiary should only be allowed in those instances where there is a time limitation regarding its corporate life and that when the period has expired it be set up as a separate company or that one of the parent companies buys out the others.

4. Assuming that the courts would issue an injunction forbidding the participating companies from continuing to engage in illegal combinations in the future, the possibility of divestiture might result in real relief. This could be accomplished by requiring the parent companies to sell their interest in the joint subsidiary and the establishment of it as an independent company or through the purchase by one of the parent companies of the interest held by the other.

5. Since the joint venture has behind it the economic power of not one but two or more companies, the pooling of their financial resources may result in the ventures obtaining an advantage over other firms in the industry. Concentration of economic power is a basis for pursuing anti-trust litigation.

6. The "conscious parallelism of action" doctrine [20] has been accepted in small measure by the courts. If this doctrine were more widely applied to partners in joint ventures, regardless of the area or industry in which this partnership exists, the simple fact that they have a joint corporate interest should suffice as a showing of collusion. Further evidence relating to their relationship would not be necessary, the only issue being left is determination of the reasonableness of the restraint.

---

[20] A tacit understanding, the existence of which may be inferred from (a) a motive for concerted action, and (b) virtual unanimity of action.

7. The scope of the present FTC prior notification regulation for mergers [21] should be extended to include the formation of new joint ventures. The inclusion of joint ventures in such a regulation is consistent with the basic premise of merger prior notification because a joint subsidiary is actually a quasi-merger.

8. Another action which might limit the onus of anti-competitive activity would be for the parent companies in a joint venture to make available to any applicant, in non-discriminatory terms, any know-how, patents or products or processes that may result from the venture. Thus the benefits of the formation of a joint venture would accrue to the parent firms, the rest of the industry, and society.

---

[21] Published initially in the Federal Register in 1969 pursuant to Section 6 of the FTC Act.

VI. DIRECTOR INTERLOCKS IN THE OIL INDUSTRY

An interlocking directorate is another aspect of an intimate relationship between corporations. To assure competition by keeping company decisions separate and preserving arms-length relationships, the Clayton Act says that "no person at the same time shall be a director in any two or more corporations . . ." who are engaged, by virtue of their business and location of operation, as competitors so that the elimination of such competition by agreement between them would constitute a violation of the antitrust laws.

Types of Interlocks

Interlockng directorships are of various types depending upon the directness of the linkage, the frequency of the linkage, and the responsibilities of the persons who constitute the links. Oil companies that are linked together may be actual or potential competitors, or buyers and sellers of crude, fractionated products, transmission services and marketing services.

The interlock may depend entirely upon a single director in each corporation, or it may consist of mutiple ties of several different directors who meet each other on several corporate boards. The more numerous the interlocks, the stronger the presumption that they create unity of action.

Corporate linkages may differ in character with the functions and responsibilities of the persons who constitute the links. The so-called professional director who is invited to take a place on various boards because of his competence to cope with particular problems of corporate management, probably is least active in co-ordinating the interest of different corporations, partly because of his personal detachment and partly because his multiple director-ships are not likely to be centered in closely-related corporations.

Representation by a high officer of the corporation may mean more than representation by a subordinate officer. A test of activity: the number of directors who hold an active position in a corpora-tion on which they serve such as chairman of the board, member of the executive committee or an executive vice president of the cor-poration. In showing relationships between various segments and levels of the oil industry, we have distinguished between "inside" and "outside" directors, arbitrarily defining "inside" and hence more active, as the chairman, president, and executive vice president of these corporations.

Interlocks may differ in the directness with which one corpora-tion meets another. The most direct and simple form of interlock is that forbidden by section 8 of the Clayton Act, in which a director of one corporation is also a director of another corporation. How-ever, even this passes over into the gray area of permissiveness if the corporations, although engaged in the manufacture and sale of identical products, operate in different geographical areas. On the other hand, if an oil company director sits on the board of a com-petitor outside the oil industry, as for example a coal company or a public utility, the interlock could be highly significant.

Similarly, if the oil company director sits on the board of a financial institution, then a whole host of relationships arise the least of which might be the conventional extension of credit. As will be shown in Chapter VII, ties to banks and other financial institu-tions are means whereby oil company management insures its own continuing control.

A question frequently asked is whether oil company executives below the director level of their company might serve as directors on other oil or oil-related companies. The answer: It happens very in-frequently. We examined a sample of 72 men, half of whom were both officers and directors of the oil companies and the remaining half were officers but not directors of the oil companies. This survey revealed that the group of officers who were not directors did not show up as directors with sufficient frequency to warrant searching their group as a whole (see appendix II for actual findings).

Oil companies may be indirectly interlocked by the fact that their dircetors sit together on the board of a third company, not otherwise affiliated with either of them. This is a secondary type of interlock.

Of course there is no clear implication that the mere presence of two or more oil company executives as directors of several corporations is of significance. Some of these relationships may be purely fortuitous and others without significance on the basis of further knowledge. However, when there is a pattern of relationships which repeats itself in kind and frequency and where it is demonstrated that the possibilities clearly exist for anti-competitive action, then the pattern should be regarded as more than circumstantial.

Interlocking Directorships Are Suspect

A board of directors has authority, under the general principles of corporation law, as representative of the owners of the company, to select the management and to determine questions of fundamental policy.

An individual who is a member of more than one board of directors cannot divide his personality into unrelated segments. When sitting on one board he necessarily continues to know what he has found out on other boards, what he has recommended to those boards, and what action those boards have taken. He would be derelict if in two different boards he supported policies, each of which would tend to defeat the course of action he had recommended or seen adopted in the other company. His duty as a director is necessarily to harmonize those interests as far as possible.

A director, whether direct or indirect, of two competing corporations cannot in good conscience recommend that either shall undertake a type of competition which is likely to injure the other.

A director of two corporations that are respectively buyer and seller of the same commodities or services cannot in good conscience recommend that either concern prefer unrelated sources of supply, instead of the other company in which he is interested, nor that concern press to the limits its ability to strike a good bargain at the expense of the other.

A director on the board of an oil company and a financial institution would find it hard in good conscience to encourage his bank to finance expansion by competitors of his oil company thereby jeopardizing its prosperity. Nor can he in good conscience encourage the oil company to obtain its credit through other channels.

If a person is a director of an oil company and a bank in which the latter is the caretaker and advisor of a pension trust fund of the former, he would feel it incumbent upon himself as a director of the bank to influence the trust department to vote those common stock holdings in favor of management of the oil company of which he is a part. Other directors on the bank board would feel it incumbent upon themselves, in order to retain the business of the oil company, to be mindful of the pressures which are brought by the director serving both companies to keep an eye out for the interest of those two companies.

Thus, the inherent tendency of interlocking directorates between companies that have dealings with each other as buyers and sellers, or of providing services, or that have relations to each other as competitors, is to blunt the edge of rivalry between them, to seek out ways of compromising opposing interests.

It is reasonable to suppose that the choice of these directors, because of the fewness of the places on a corporate board, is not inadvertent. However, even if there was no purpose in the selection, the tendency to harmonize conflicting interests is built into the functions of such directors.

Sources Of Data

The technique of studying anti-competitive action over the years has frequently found a handmaiden in the use of interlocking directorates. It played an outstanding role at the close of the Thirties when the Temporary National Economic Committee (TNEC) undertook and completed its monumental studies on the economic structure of the country.

This study has drawn upon prior experience in appraising interlocking directorates, but with one notable difference. Most studies started with a universe of firms irrespective of industry, frequently the first 100 largest firms or 500 largest firms or perhaps even 1,000 largest firms. This study was more selective. It set out to explore as one of its major approaches the acquisition by oil companies of competing energy firms. It subsequently broadened after discovery that a new dimension was introduced when relationships were explored with financial institutions. Therefore, the list of firms from which interlocking directorates were drawn are as follows:

1. The thirty-two largest oil companies of 1971 as defined in Fortune's 500. This included British Petroleum because of its close ties to Standard Oil of Ohio.
2. The twenty-five largest coal companies taken from the Keystone Coal Industry Manual and based on 1971 production.
3. The nineteen largest utilities of 1971 from Fortune's list of 50 largest utilities.
4. The twenty largest investment companies, again based on Fortune's list.
5. The twenty largest life insurance companies based on Fortune's list.
6. The seven largest oil foundations, in terms of assets, based on data from the Foundation Library.
7. The twenty largest banks based on the Fortune directory.
8. The nineteen largest U.S. crude oil pipelines based on revenues and taken from the Interstate Commerce Commission's Transport Statistics, 1971.
9. The twenty-one largest U.S. gas pipelines from the Federal Power Commission.
10. Six of the largest uranium companies supplied by the Atomic Energy Commission.

Less than a handful of exceptions were made. Burlington Northern and Union Pacific owned the largest coal reserves in the country and their boards were added.

In total, there were 193 firms in our sample, but they were the goliaths in their respective industries. These companies had a total of 2,619 directors and it was among them that we examined for interlocking relationships. If other industrial establishments had been included, the additional data would probably show more vertical integration between the oil industry and these other firms both back to their sources of supply and forward to their customers.

Starting with firm names, the directors were taken from Standard and Poor's Directory of Corporation Directors and Executives, 1971 and updated via supplements through September 1972.

THE FINDINGS

Primary Interlocks Between Oil Companies

1. Overlapping directorates between oil companies.—There appears to be at least one direct violation of the Clayton Act by virtue of one director—H. A. Shepard—who is on the boards of both Standard Oil of Ohio and Diamond Shamrock Corporation. It may well be that because the areas in which these two companies operate are exclusive of one another that they do not fall within the scope of the Clayton Act.

2. Overlapping directorates between oil companies and other energy companies.—While there were a significant number of interlocks between oil and coal companies, in many instances these merely reflected the fact that the latter were owned by the former. In four instances, however, oil companies were associated with coal companies not owned by them:

1. Commonwealth Oil Refining and Amax—I. K. McGregor
2. Diamond Shamrock and General Dynamics—W. R. Persons
3. Standard of Ohio and Republic Steel—C. E. Spahr
4. Marathon Oil and Republic Steel—W. B. Boyer

Both Amax and General Dynamics, the former a subsidiary of American Metal Climax and the other the parent company of Freeman United Electric, are both major producers of coal with output of some 12 million tons each in 1971. In addition, Amax Coal is reported to have 4 billion tons of estimated reserves of which about half is in low sulphur coal. Republic Steel produces 4 million tons of coal most probably for its own use. Marketing territories for both Standard of Ohio and Marathon are in, or close to, the states in which Republic Steel has its major operations. In addition, both Marathon and Sohio sell gasoline in Ohio. In both the Standard of Ohio and Marathon situations, the overlapping director is an "active" officer in one of the firms.

Oil and utility direct overlaps exist between 5 major oil companies and 5 major utilities around the country as follows:

Commonwealth Oil Refining and Middle South Utilities—
G. F. Bennett

Mobil and Consolidated Edison—G. L. Kirk

Standard of Indiana and Commonwealth Edison—J. S. Wright

Standard of Ohio and Detroit Edison—P. W. McCracken

Getty Oil and Southern California Edison—F. G. Larkin, Jr.

The utility industry as a whole is under great pressure from environmentalists to switch to low sulphur coal or natural gas because their emissions are least harmful to the environment. The oil companies are crucially involved in decisions in which their major customers are in the market for coal, crude oil, natural gas, or nuclear power. It would be interesting to observe how these overlapping directors harmonize the interests of their respective companies as well as with those of consumers.

Chapter III reveals the major inroads by the oil industry into the uranium, mining and milling industry. These inroads reflected ownership and that appears to be the most popular type of liaison between oil and uranium. One relationship, other than ownership, is the overlapping directorship between Marathon Oil and Anaconda Copper, the latter an owner of a uranium facility. Mr. J. B. Place serves on the board of both of these companies and is an active or inside director of Anaconda.

The popularity of joint ventures as a means of transporting crude petroleum and its derivatives has been remarked on elsewhere in this study. These ventures are so numerous and are characterized by such intimate working relationships that is hardly necessary to achieve closeness by other means. Consequently, the incidence of overlapping directorships in the transmission of crude petroleum was confined to only one instance and a parent-subsidiary one at that —the Union Oil Company of California and the Pure Transportation Company. Mr. C. S. Brinegar, currently the Secretary of Transportation, was a director in both of these companies and an active one in each.

There were two instances of oil companies sharing a director with a natural gas transmission company. American Petrofina and Northern Natural Gas share a director—Mr. S. F. Silloway. As might be expected, Eastern Gas and Fuel Associates shared two directors—Mr. E. Goldston and J. N. Phillips—with its subsidiary, the Algonquin Gas Transmission Company.

There were other examples of overlapping directorships but they were parent-subsidiary relationships. These included Consolidation Coal and Continental Oil, British Petroleum and Standard Oil of Ohio, Tenneco and Midwestern Gas Transmission Company, Phillips Petroleum and Colonial Pipeline, the latter a joint venture in which Phillips is involved.

3. Overlapping directorates between oil companies and financial institutions.—If there was one outstanding fact emerging from the welter of corporate relationships in the oil industry, that fact would have to be the hand-in-glove association of oil companies with financial institutions, particularly banks.

A network of 14 banks was tied to 18 of the largest oil companies. On the basis of interlocks, the institutions shown in Table 23 might popularly be regarded as oil banks (one overlapping director each except where otherwise indicated in parenthesis).

Table 23.
Director Interlocks: Selected Banks and Oil Companies, 1972

Continental Illinois Nat'l Bank & Trust
    Continental Oil
  (2) Standard of Indiana
    Texaco
    Universal Oil Products

Chase Manhattan
    Atlantic Richfield
    Diamond Shamrock
    Exxon
    Standard of Indiana

Chemical Bank
  (2) Amerada Hess
  (2) Exxon
    Mobil
    Texaco

Morgan Guaranty Trust
    Cities Service
    Continental Oil
    Atlantic Richfield
    Exxon

First National City Bank
    Phillips
    Mobil
    Shell

Bankers Trust
    Continental
    Mobil

Bank of America
    Standard of California
  (2) Union Oil
  (2) Getty

Western Bancorporation
  (2) Standard of Calif.
    Union Oil

Mellon Nat'l Bank & Trust
  (3) Gulf
    Diamond Shamrock

First National Boston
  (2) Commonwealth Oil
    Refining

Manufacturers Hanover
    Cities Service

Crocker National
    Standard of Calif.

Security Pacific
    Kerr-McGee
    Getty

First Chicago
    Atlantic Richfield

Chart VI. Interlocking Directorates:
Largest Oil Companies and Largest Banks, 1972

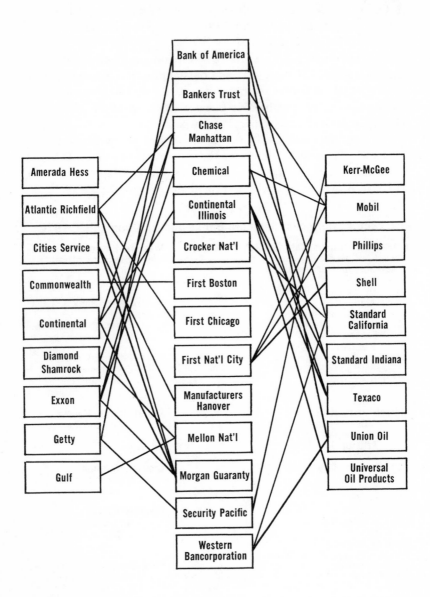

While the overlaps by themselves would indicate a community of interest, it is also noteworthy how other oil companies are brought together via secondary bank interlocks (Chart VI). The banks could

Table 24. Interlocking Directorates: Selected Oil Industry and Financial Institutions,[1] October 1972

Company	Banks	Insurance	Investment
Amer. Petrofina..	....	....	I.D.S.
Amerada Hess....	(2)Chemical	(2)Mutual Bnft. Life New York Life	....
Cities Service.....	Mfrs. Hanover Morgan Guaranty	Mutual of N.Y.	....
Atlantic Rich......	Chase-Manhattan Morgan Guaranty First Chicago	(2)Penn Mutual Life	Chubb
Continental Oil...	Bankers Trust Continental, Ill. Morgan Guaranty	Equitable Life	....
Commonwealth..	First Nat'l Bost.	John Hancock	....
East. Gas & Fuel..	....	John Hancock	....
Exxon............	Chase-Manhattan (2)Chemical........ Morgan Guaranty	Prudential	St. Paul Cos.
Diamond Sham...	Chase-Manhattan Mellon Nat'l		CIT Financial
Getty.............	(2)Bank of America. Security-Pacific	....	....
Marathon.........	....	New York Life	....
Gulf.............	(3)Mellon Nat'l	....	....
Kerr McGee......	Security-Pacific	....	....
Parker Hannifin..	....	....	Financial Fed.
Phillips...........	First Nat'l City	....	....
Mobil............	Bankers Trust First Nat'l City Chemcial	Metropolitan	Transamerica Finan. American Expr.
Standard Calif....	Bank of America Crocker Nat'l (2)West. Bancorp.	Prudential	....
Standard Indiana.	(2)Continental Ill. Chase-Manhattan	....	Household Fin.
Shell.............	First Nat'l City	Conn. Mutual	....
Signal............	....	....	CNA Financial
Union Oil.........	(2)Bank of America West. Bancorp.	....	....
U.O.P.............	Continental Ill.	N. Western Mutual	....
Texaco...........	Continental Ill. Chemical	Mutual of N.Y.	....

[1] Foundations are not shown in listing. Gulf had an interlocking directorate with the Mellon (Richard King) Foundation and Texaco with the Rockefeller Foundation.

be the perfect conduit for an exchange of information or parallel action with respect to these "competitors".

Moreover, as will be seen in Chapter VII, the cement is further hardened by the pension funds which oil companies place in the care of these banks, the trust funds over which banks exercise fiduciary decisions, and the very competition for oil company business itself so that the ability to avoid conflict of interest or anti-competitive actions becomes a difficult problem for all.

Primary interlocks do not stop at banks. Insurance companies, investment companies and foundations also control great financial resources and wield commensurate power. While their joint relationships are not as pervasive, nor even as powerful, as banks, they are part of the apparatus of control. Thirteen oil companies have at least one director in common with an insurance company and eight oil companies have interlocks with investment companies (Table 24).

Secondary Interlocks

Attention thus far has been directed at primary interlocks. It is only when second level overlaps are added that one can appreciate the full capacity for joint action.

Perhaps the best way to demonstrate the nature and complexity of interlocking directorates and the possibility for joint action is to show the pattern for Continental Oil. True, Continental is somewhat more gregarious than most but the differences are slight.

Listed immediately below is an illustration of how this company reaches into other energy areas and how financial institutions provide the glue which holds them all together.

Continental Oil Company

Banks	**—Bankers Trust Company**
Insurance	—Mutual of New York
Insurance	—Prudential Ins. Co. of America
Coal	—Consolidation Coal Company
Investments	—American Express Company
Foundations	—Commonwealth Fund
Foundations	—Rockefeller Foundation
Oil	—Mobil Oil Corp.

Banks	**—Cont'ent Ill. Nat. B&T Co., Chicago**
Banks	—Northwest Bancorporation
Insurance	—Aetna Life & Casualty
Coal	—Consolidation Coal Company
Coal	—General Dynamics Corp.
(2) Utilities	—Commonwealth Edison
(2) Oil	—Standard Oil Co.—Indiana
Oil	—Universal Oil Products Co.
Oil	—Texaco Inc.
Banks	**—Morgan Guaranty Trust Co. of N.Y.**
(2) Insurance	—Aetna Life and Casualty
Insurance	—John Hancock Mutual Life Ins. Co.
Insurance	—Metropolitan Life Ins. Co.
Insurance	—Penn Mutual Life Ins. Co.
Coal	—Burlington Northern Inc.
(2) Coal	—United States Steel Corp.
(2) Investment	—INA Corporation
Investment	—Chubb Corp.
Uranium	—Union Carbide Corp.
Gas Pipelines	—Panhandle Eastern Pipeline Co.
Utilities	—Duke Power Co.
Utilities	—Niagara Mohawk Power Corp.
Oil	—Cities Service Co.
Oil	—Atlantic Richfield
Oil	—Standard Oil Co.—New Jersey
Insurance	**—Equitable Life Assurance Soc. of the U.S.**
Banks	—Chase Manhattan Bank
Banks	—Mellon National Bank & Trust
(2) Banks	—Chemical Bank
(2) Insurance	—Equitable Life Assurance Soc. of the U.S.
Coal	—Burlington Northern Inc.
Coal	—United Steel Corp.
(2) Foundations	—Rockefeller Foundation
Uranium	—Rio Algom Mines Ltd.
Utilities	—American Electric Power (NY)
Utilities	—Commonwealth Edison
Utilities	—Consolidated Edison
(3) Coal	**—Consolidation Coal Company**
Banks	—Cont'ent Ill. Nat. B&T Co., Chicago
(2) Coal	—Mathais Coal Company
Uranium	—Union Carbide Corporation
Gas Pipelines	—Northern Natural Gas Company
Utilities	—American Electric Power (NY)
(1) Coal	**—Mathias Coal Company**
Banks	—National Bank of Detroit

The interpretation of the above listing is as follows: Continental Oil has one overlapping director with Bankers Trust Company. Bankers Trust in turn has overlapping directors with 2 insurance companies, one investment company, and 2 oil foundations. In the energy field Bankers Trust has an overlapping directorship with a coal company and an oil company.

Continental also has one overlapping director with the Continental Illinois National Bank and Trust Company. The latter

has overlaps with one bank, one insurance company, two coal companies, a large utility and three oil companies.

Continental has yet another joint director with still a third bank, Morgan Guaranty Trust Company. This colossus of the financial world in turn has overlapping directorships with four insurance companies, two coal companies, two investment companies, one uranium company, one gas pipeline, two utilities, and three oil companies.

Leaving the banking field, Continental has an overlap with the Equitable Life Insurance Society. And what friends does this mammoth insurance company make? Merely director relationships with three banks, one insurance company, two coal companies, one oil foundation, a uranium company and three utilities.

Continental Oil also owns the Consolidation Coal Company and shares three directors with it. Who else sits on the Consolidation Coal board? Merely a director of the Continental Illinois bank and directors from three other energy industries.

Finally, on the board of Mathias Coal Company, which is a

subsidiary of Consolidation, there sits a representative of the National Bank of Detroit.

In summary, the possibilities for interchange of ideas or parallel action almost defy comprehension. Continental Oil has direct overlaps with three banks; one insurance company, and two coal companies, among many others. Indirectly, these six companies have secondary overlaps with seven of the country's largest insurance companies, five of the largest coal companies, two investment companies, two foundations, seven other oil companies, five banks, five of the largest utilities in the country, two uranium companies, and two gas pipelines.

Coal, uranium, utilities. These are the three energy forms competitive with the oil industry. Yet we see for a single company how the tentacles reach out and encompass such a huge segment of American industrial power.

Multiply this network for a single company by other larger oil companies and the concentration of power appears overwhelming. (Appendix III lists primary and secondary interlocks of our largest oil companies with other energy and financial institutions only.)

It is not surprising, therefore, that a certain unanimity of action emanates from the oil industry. Self-serving advertisements on how they are safe-guarding the ecology, helping the small businessman, and straining to meet the Nation's energy needs are in counterpoint to their threats to slow exploration, refusal to provide information on natural gas reserves, pleas for deregulation and reduced oil quotas to small independent competitors. Amidst this cacophony of sound emerges a single passage: Higher prices to the consumer.

The questions begging a reply are the extent to which a conscious parallelism of action exists in the industry fostered by first and second level overlapping directorships and the degree of tolerance by the government in permitting such overlaps to exist in competing energy forms.

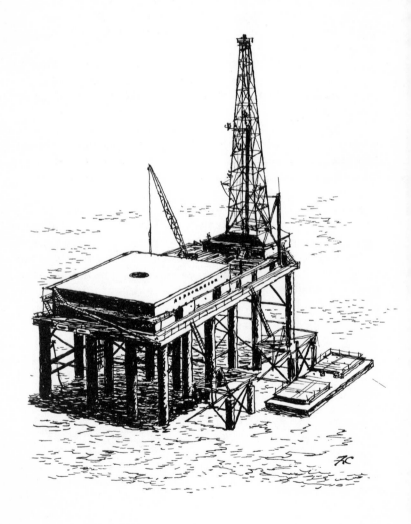

VII. OIL COMPANIES AND FINANCIAL INSTITUTIONS

The close relationship between oil companies and certain financial institutions is a fundamental fact of corporate life. It is the binding which pulls together the disparate pieces of the energy industries outside the capital structures of the oil companies. It provides the means, should it be needed, for oil company management to perpetuate itself in power. It insures the flow of financial services which occupy an increasingly large share of modern corporation activities. It sets up the means to provide an information and policy conduit between oil companies and electric and gas utilities, the latter perhaps the largest single customer for petroleum and gas supplies. Moreover, there is always the concern that banks and other financial institutions which hold large blocks of oil stocks may act in concert, by aggregating their interests to achieve common objectives.

Financial institutions as defined here include banks, insurance companies, investment companies and foundations. Also included are the managing underwriters, those prestigious banking houses who lead financial consortiums in raising hundreds of millions of dollars of debt capital for the oil industry.

Relatively little is known of the relationships between oil companies and financial institutions. Bank trust departments, which control enormous sums of money of non-financial institutions, have hidden for years behind the device of confidentiality of trust information. A technique known as a nominee account permits institutions with large blocks of stocks to conceal their holdings by placing them under a meaningless name and using these names to satisfy disclosure requirements.[22] Brokerage firms have refused information on voting and ownership on blocks of stock in many corporations. Subpoena powers have often become embroiled in a maze of legal action which tends to negate the power of the subpoena itself.

Less than a handful of investigations of bank financial activities

---

[22] Senator Lee Metcalf, Montana, unraveled this device by causing to be printed in the Congressional Record, June 24, 1971, the list of nominee accounts and their respective owners.

have been conducted in recent times and these largely on a one-time basis. There is the famous study conducted by the Committee on Banking and Currency of the House of Representatives and frequently referred to as "The Patman" after its illustrious chairman.[23] This study enjoys particular lustre because in addition to making a series of conclusions it also reveals specific bank names and their related corporate clients.

The Securities and Exchange Commission, in 1971, also released a monumental report broader in scope than the Patman. It covered the entire institutional investment field of banks, insurance, investment, off-shore funds, foundations, educational endowments and pension-benefit plans. Unlike the previously mentioned House study, it did not identify individual institutional holdings.[24]

These and other studies reveal in part the manner in which financial institutions and the oil industry enjoy a relationship which inures to the benefit of both. It explains the protective attitudes toward one another, common areas of interest and the means whereby common goals can be established.

The Financial and Oil Industry Fraternity

How do institutions maintain close alliances and working relations with oil companies? The techniques are manifold.

1. Interlocking directors between financial institutions and oil companies is a major tool. The extent to which these relationships exist is shown in Chapter VI of this volume.

2. Banks, insurance companies and investment companies through their marshalling of vast sums of money are purchasers of common stock of many of the oil companies.

3. Banks exercise the potential for an enormous amount of control within the oil industry through employee benefit funds. Of the approximately 11,000 such funds for all industries in 1967, some four-fifths give the banks sole voting rights over all stock investments. Thus, as these employee benefits funds continue to grow

[23] "Commercial Banks and Their Trust Activities: Emerging Influence on the American Economy", Committee on Banking and Currency, House of Representatives, 90th Congress, 2nd Session, July 1968, two volumes.

[24] Institutional Investor Study Report of the Securities and Exchange Commission (House Document 92-64), March 10, 1971.

at a rapid rate and the funds continue to be invested heavily in common equities, the banks' power to influence, control, or act in unison or harmony with management of corporations through the voting of stock also increases substantively.

4. Certain banks are known as "oil banks". This is because they either share directors with oil companies, provide short term money, manage their employee benefit funds, or hold a significant proportion of the outstanding stock of the corporation. The extent to which a bank furnishes funds to the oil industry may be a cause or outgrowth of the close relationship described above. By virtue of their control of large blocks of common stock in oil companies, these banks or other financial institutions can influence stock prices of the oil companies and have an input into oil company corporate policy.

5. Because of the heavy stake of financial institutions in the oil industry and the commonality of interest which it fosters, banks may frequently act as a conduit of information and corporate policy from one oil company to another. Also possible is the extension of the conduit in which the bank may pursue oil industry interests vis-a-vis the energy industries. Financial institutions provide great sums of money to public utilities, coal companies and other industries in the corporate spectrum. The motivation to act for the "common good" is very strong.

6. Banks also play a significant role in corporate mergers. They are likely to enter into a considerable amount of decision making, determining the conditions for bringing the companies together and for issuing new securities, and may also choose, or participate in choosing, the directors and chief execuitves who are to head the new company. The voting power of banks' trust departments is another factor in approving corporate mergers.

Potential Areas of Conflict

These means of corporate influence or control are not without hazard since they can involve potential conflicts of interest. On the one hand a very large financial institution with directors or funds committed to two or more oil companies might find it very difficult or even impossible to remain equally loyal to both beneficiaries. Would it therefore follow that the bank would do all in its means to harmonize relationships of the two companies so that neither one is threatened?

One of the more serious potential conflict-of-interest problems arises where a pension fund purchases and votes the stock of the corporation which created the fund. The obvious conflict in such situation is that management is able to perpetuate itself in office indefinitely. Of course there are certain exceptions. Exxon in 1957, established the practice of permitting employees covered under its Alternate fund to themselves vote the company stock held in that fund. To what extent does this "pass through" exist with respect to all funds in Exxon or indeed in the pension funds of other oil companies? It is believed that most companies do not provide for such a pass through of voting rights.

What about the bank trustee who is supposedly managing the pension fund for benefit of the company's employees? If the company is a good customer of the bank and the trustee account consists of many shares of that corporation, is the bank's trust department likely to sell shares of the company if that is the proper investment decision to make, thus jeopardizing not only its business relationship with the company but also the manner in which both the company and the bank exercise continuing control over the corporation?

The bank officer who sits on the board of an oil company is also in a privileged position to get inside information. He may use this knowledge to make decisions about his trustee accounts but at the same time he has a responsibility to the company on whose board he sits to act in its best interests. Can he faithfully serve two masters and if not, which does he serve?

After The Possibilities, What Are The Involvements?

Commercial banks and the oil industry.—Information on commercial bank activities, their investment decisions, their relationships to specific corporations, their trust department activities, and their corporate policy as reflected in general investment decisions is not available to the public. This makes it extremely difficult to ferret out the relationship of commercial banks to industry in general and to the oil industry in particular.

However, revealing facts surfaced about the ties between the oil companies and commercial banks. That the information is some five years old appears of little consequences since many of the old relationships proved quite enduring. In the single aspect in which comparisons can be made between 1967 and 1972—director interlocks—the pattern has a certain marked resemblance. The disappearance of certain corporate oil names (Sinclair, Sunray DX) and the changing character of the 30 largest limits the comparison somewhat. Nevertheless, the tried and tested bank affiliations are present in force—Chase Manhattan, First National City, Bankers Trust, Chemical, Continental Illinois and Morgan Guaranty. Significantly, the most enduring relationship occurred where oil company employee benefit funds were managed by banks in 1967. In all such instances except one, the oil companies maintained an interlocking director into 1972 (although it is not known whether supervision over the benefit fund was continued).

Moreover, there is no reason to expect an upheaval in relationships between Chase Manhattan and the oil companies over five years with a Rockefeller still in charge of Chase Manhattan. Similarly, the Mellon National Bank, holding a large share of Gulf stock, would be unlikely to divest itself of that kind of relationship.

The 1967 Congressional study had specific information on 19 major oil companies. Reference to Table 25, shows that for the 19 oil companies listed there were 48 primary director interlocks.

Eleven of these 19 firms had employee benefit funds managed by 9 major banks. The distribution of these managed employee benefit funds was as follows:

Bank	Number of Oil Company Employee Benefit Funds Managed, 1967
Chase-Manhattan, N.Y.	2
First Nat'l City, N.Y.	8
Bankers Trust, N.Y.	2
Chemical Bank, N.Y.	2
Mellon Nat'l Bank, Pitts.	10
First Nat'l Bank, Chicago	2
Morgan Guaranty, N.Y.	2
Philadelphia Nat'l, Phila.	1
Nat'l City of Cleveland	2

Table 25. Stockholder, Directorship and Employee Benefit Fund Links of 49 Banks Surveyed With Petroleum Refining Companies, 1967

Name of company	Name of bank	Director interlocks	Employee benefit funds managed by bank	Voting arrangements				
				Stock type [1]	Total percent of out- standing stock	Per- cent sole vote [2]	Per- cent partial vote [3]	Per- cent no vote [4]
Standard Oil Co., N.J.	Chase Manhattan Bank, New York, N.Y.	2	1	.....	.....	.....	.....	.....
	First Nat'l City Bank, New York, N.Y.	1	1	.....	.....	.....	.....	.....
Total		3	2	.....	.....	.....	.....	.....
Mobil Oil Corp.	First Nat'l Bank of Boston, Mass.	1		.....	.....	.....	.....	.....
	First Nat'l City Bank, New York, N.Y.	2		.....	.....	.....	.....	.....
	Bankers Trust Co., New York, N.Y.	1	2	.....	.....	.....	.....	.....
Total		4	2	.....	.....	.....	.....	.....
Texaco, Inc.	Nat'l City Bank of Cleveland, Ohio	1		.....	.....	.....	.....	.....
	Chemcial Bank New York Trust, N.Y., N.Y.	2	2	.....	.....	.....	.....	.....
	Union Nat'l Bank of Pittsburgh, Pa.	1		.....	.....	.....	.....	.....
Total		4	2	.....	.....	.....	.....	.....

Table 25. Stockholder, Directorship and Employee Benefit Fund Links of 49 Banks Surveyed With Petroleum Refining Companies, 1967 (Cont'd)

Name of company	Name of bank	Director interlocks	Employee benefit funds managed by bank	Stock type [1]	Voting arrangements			
					Total percent of outstanding stock	Percent sole vote [2]	Percent partial vote [3]	Percent no vote [4]
Gulf Oil Corp.	Mellon Nat'l Bank & Trust, Pittsburgh, Pa.	4	10	C	17.1	1.9	10.8	4.4
Shell Oil Co.	First Nat'l Bank of Chicago, Ill.	1						
	Hartford Nat'l Bank & Trust, Hartford, Conn.	1						
Total		2						
Standard Oil Co., Indiana	Union Trust Co. of Maryland, Baltimore, Md.	1						
	Continental Ill. Nat'l Bank, Chicago, Ill.	1						
	First Nat'l Bank of Chicago, Ill.	2	2	C	7.7	1.1	0.3	6.3
	Harris Trust & Savings Bank, Chicago, Ill.	1						
	American Nat'l Bank & Trust, Chicago, Ill.	1	1					
	Chase Manhattan Bank, N.A., New York, N.Y.	1						
Total		7	3	C	7.7	1.1	.3	6.3

Table 25. Stockholder, Directorship and Employee Benefit Fund Links of 49 Banks Surveyed With Petroleum Refining Companies, 1967 (Cont'd)

Name of company	Name of bank	Director interlocks	Employee benefit funds managed by bank	Stock type [1]	Total percent of outstanding stock	Percent sole vote [2]	Percent partial vote [3]	Percent no vote [4]
Continental Oil Co.,	Continental Ill. Nat'l Bank, Chicago, Ill.	1	....	....	....	....	....	....
	Morgan Guaranty Trust Co., New York, N.Y.	2	1	....	....	....	....	....
	Bankers Trust Co., New York, N.Y.	2	....	....	....	....	....	....
Total	....	5	1	....	....	....	....	....
Phillips Petroleum Co.,	First Nat'l City Bank, New York, N.Y.	....	6	C	6.6	.1	.1	6.4
Sinclair Oil Corp.,	First Nat'l City Bank New York, N.Y.	2	1	....	....	....	....	....
Union Oil of California	Continental Ill. Nat'l Bank, Chicago, Ill.	1	....	....	....	....	....	....
	Northern Trust Co., Chicago, Ill.	1	....	....	....	....	....	....
Total	....	2	....	....	....	....	....	....

Table 25. Stockholder, Directorship and Employee Benefit Fund Links of 49 Banks Surveyed With Petroleum Refining Companies, 1967 (Cont'd)

Name of company	Name of bank	Director interlocks	Employee benefit funds managed by bank	Stock type[1]	Voting arrangements			
					Total percent of outstanding stock	Percent sole vote[2]	Percent partial vote[3]	Percent no vote[4]
Cities Service Co...	Morgan Guaranty Trust Co., New York, N.Y.	1	1					
	Chemical Bank New York Trust, New York, N.Y.	1						
Total...		2	1					
Atlantic Richfield Co...	Morgan Guaranty Trust Co. New York, N.Y.	1						
	First Penn. Bank & Trust, Phila., Pa.	1						
	Girard Trust Co., Phila., Pa.	1						
	Union Nat'l Bank of Pittsburgh, Pa.			P	8.3		4.0	
Total...		3		P	8.3	4.3	4.0	
Sun Oil Co...	Philadelphia Nat'l Bank, Phila., Pa.		1	C	6.3	6.3		
Marathon Oil Co...	Nat'l City Bank of Cleveland, Ohio	2	1					

99

Table 25. Stockholder, Directorship and Employee Benefit Fund Links of 49 Banks Surveyed With Petroleum Refining Companies, 1967 (Cont'd)

Name of company	Name of bank	Director interlocks	Employee benefit funds managed by bank	Stock type[1]	Voting arrangements			
					Total percent of outstanding stock	Percent sole vote[2]	Percent partial vote[3]	Percent no vote[4]
Standard Oil Co., Ohio	Nat'l City Bank of Cleveland, Ohio	3	1	P	31.0	31.0	.....	.....
				C	6.1	5.9	.....	.2
	Central Nat'l Bank of Cleveland, Ohio	2						
Total		5	1	P	31.0	31.0	.....	.....
				C	6.1	5.9	.....	.2
Sunray DX Oil Company	Pittsburgh Nat'l Bank, Pittsburgh, Pa.	1						
Kerr McGee Corp.	State Street Bank & Trust, Boston, Mass.			C	10.1	.3	.....	9.8
Murphy Oil Corp.	Fidelity Bank, Phila., Pa.	2						
Pennzoil Co.	State Street Bank & Trust, Boston, Mass.			C	7.7	.....	.....	7.7

Footnotes to Table 25

[1] The letter "C" designates a common or capital stock issue. The letter "P" designates an issue of stock other than a common or capital stock issue. Where more than one "P" appears under one bank's holdings, in most cases this indicates the holding of several different kinds of preferred stock.

[2] "Sole voting right": A bank is considered to have sole voting right—(a) Where an officer or officers of the bank have the right to vote the stock without consulting persons not connected with the bank; (b) Where officers or directors of the bank constitute a majority of the board of directors, trustees, or other governing body of a pension plan, profit-sharing plan, or foundation, and where such majority has the power to determine how the shares held by such plan or foundation are to be voted.

[3] "Partial voting right": A bank is considered to have partial voting right—(a) Where the bank or its nominee is a cotrustee or coexecutor and votes in concert with another trustee or executor; (b) Where the bank or its nominee may proceed to vote the stock, if after notifying someone else, it is not given instructions on how to vote; (c) Where the bank or its nominee submits recommendations to the beneficial owner on how to vote the stock; (d) Where the officers or directors of the bank constitute less than a majority of the board of directors, trustees, or other governing body of a pension plan, profit-sharing plan, or foundation, and where such board of directors, trustees, or other governing body has the power to determine how the shares held by such plan or foundation are to be voted.

[4] "No voting right": A bank is considered to have no voting right where the beneficial owner or some other person or entity not connected with the bank has the sole right to vote the stock.

* The Standard Industrial Classification designates the principal products manufactured or the major services furnished by each company. These classifications were prepared by the Technical Committee on Standard Industrial Classification, under the sponsorship and supervision of the Office of Statistical Standards of the Bureau of the Budget, Executive Office of the President.

Source: *Commercial Banks and Their Trust Activities: Emerging Influence on the American Economy, Committee on Banking and Currency, House of Representatives, July 8, 1968.*

Not only did these commercial banks manage 31 employee benefit funds but in almost every instance the oil companies, as if to insure that nothing was left to chance, had an interlocking director. Such is the nature of this financial camaradarie where the stakes are high and the chances for challenge may need to be minimized accordingly.

Table 25, also shows the percent of outstanding stock of oil companies held by various banks (percentages shown only when in excess of 6%).

Senator James Couzens of Michigan used to say that whoever held 2 or 3 percent of the stock of a corporation could usually get "the majority to do the wishes of the minority". He spoke from experience half a century ago as president of the Bank of Detroit and a director of Detroit Trust. Congressman Wright Patman's House Banking Subcommittee on Domestic Finance considers 5 percent significant when judging the potential influence that a bank trust department's stockholding may have on a particular corporation, but emphasizes that "even 1 or 2 percent of stock in a publicly held corporation can gain tremendous influence over a company's policies and operations." [25]

Because common stock is widely held, an institution with only a small percentage may nevertheless be the biggest stockholder. Control can be exercised through interlocking directorates or credit policy. The most fundamental control is through voting of stock, thereby selecting the corporations' leadership and setting the general policy.

Control as reflected in stock ownership (in Table 25) tells only part of the story. Frequently, a single financial institution may not control sufficient shares by itself to exercise a compelling role. In that case two or more institutions, if their holdings were combined, could exert dominance. While such aggregation may disclose potential economic power, it need not permit the inference that institutions will act together. Nevertheless, neither can one rule out its possibility.[26]

---

[25] Notice of Hearings on Corporate Secrecy: The Nominee List—Unmasking Corporate Ownership by Senator Lee Metcalf and Vic Reinemer, Congressional Record, June 19, 1972.

[26] In the recent Equity Fund scandal (April 1973) certain investors were given prior knowledge of the Fund's difficulty. It is revealed that three banks,

The concentrated stock power of financial institutions in the oil industry is shown in Table 26. Mighty Exxon, with some 224 million shares, has at least 2½ percent of them held by one institution and at least 5 percent held by three of them. Only two institutions, separately, hold at least 5 percent of Texaco, Mobil, and Amerada Hess shares. Even more ominous, a single institution, separately, holds at least 5 percent of the outstanding shares of Gulf, Standard of California, Standard of Indiana, Phillips, and Diamond Shamrock. This incredible concentration of stock of our own oil industry in a handful of institutions should have the most profound impact on future Government antitrust activities!

"All shares held" in Table 26 is an indication of concentration without regard to whether the institution has any voting authority over the shares it holds but over which it does have some investment discretion. Perhaps a sharper measure of control is reflected in Table 27, which shows the same information as in Table 26, but with the following difference: The institutions holding the shares have sole discretion in how they vote the shares. Under this configuration, control is spread over a larger number of institutions.

Commercial Banks and Utilities.—What about the relationships of banks to public utilities, producers of competing forms of energy, and at the same major customers for oil and gas?

In the Chapter on "Interlocking Directorates" and in Appendix III, there was a clear indication of the primary interlocks between banks and oil companies and between banks and public utilities. Because the most fundamental control is through voting of stock, however, it is pertinent to examine the nature of bank stockholdings in public utilities.

The Patman study revealed that commercial banks held a substantial percentage of the outstanding stock of 92 electric and gas utilities in 1967. In 27 of them, the banks exercised sole or partial voting rights of a nature that might presume total or partial control. This voting control was supplemented by 192 overlapping directorships.

Obviously sensitive to the implications, banks make herculean

major holders of Equity stock and clients of the same investment advisor who was privy to advance information, unloaded their stock on three successive days. The oddity is that none of the banks disposed of its stock on the same day as did the others.

Table 26. Number of Institutions[1] Necessary Before All Shares Held[2] Constitute Given Percentages of the Outstanding Shares of Selected Oil Companies, September 30, 1969

Company	Percentage Of Shares Outstanding							Total Number Holding Shares
	1.0	2.5	5.0	10.0	15.0	20.0	25.0	
Exxon	1	1	3	6	13	27	49	191
Texaco	1	1	2	5	11	21	36	174
Gulf	1	1	1	1	1	2	3	163
Mobil	1	1	2	5	11	19	33	163
Stand. of Calif	1	1	1	4	10	20	37	139
Atlantic-Rich	1	2	4	8	15	23	41	156
Stand. Indiana	1	1	1	2	6	13	25	140
Phillips	1	1	1	5	13	25	53	114
Tenneco	1	5	17	—	—	—	—	81
Occidental	1	2	9	—	—	—	—	85
Amerada Hess	1	1	2	7	—	—	—	55
Diamond Shamrock	1	1	1	4	13	—	—	66

See Table 27 for footnotes.

Table 27. Number of Institutions[1] Necessary Before Shares Voted Solely[3] Constitute Given Percentages of the Outstanding Shares of Selected Oil Companies, September 30, 1969

Company	1.0	2.5	5.0	10.0	15.0	20.0	25.0	Total
Exxon	1	3	7	26	65	—	—	191
Texaco	1	2	6	17	38	95	—	174
Gulf	1	1	1	1	2	3	10	163
Mobil	1	2	4	12	29	64	—	163
Stand. of Calif	1	3	8	22	63	—	—	139
Atlantic-Rich	1	2	4	12	25	61	—	156
Stand. Indiana	1	1	1	3	10	28	98	140
Phillips	1	1	1	5	20	77	—	114
Tenneco	2	5	38	—	—	—	—	81
Occidental	1	3	33	—	—	—	—	85
Amerada Hess	1	1	2	11	—	—	—	55
Diamond Shamrock	1	1	2	7	13	—	—	66

[1] Institutions defined as Bank Trust Departments, Investment Advisors, Insurance companies and self administered funds.

[2] "All Shares Held" is an indication of concentration without regard to whether the institution has any voting authority over the shares it holds but over which it does have some investment discretion.

[3] "Shares Voted Solely" is a direct mechanism available to institutions for the purpose of influencing management and of affecting the outcome of matters submitted to shareholders for their approval.

Source: Institutional Investor Study Report of the Securities and Exchange Commission, Volume V of House Document No. 92-64.

efforts to conceal their control over public utilities. Through the nominee device which permits them to report ownership in random names, their influence among utilities is of an encompassing nature. The 1970, ownership reports of electric utilities, used in conjunction with the nominee list,[27] show that 14 banks are each among the 10 top stockholders of 10 or more utilities.

Chase Manhattan Bank, using four different names, appears among the top 10 stockholders of 42 utilities.

Morgan Guaranty Trust, using 13 different nominees, appears among the top 10 of 41 utilities.

Manufacturers Hanover Trust, using five different nominees, appears among the top 10 of 31 utilities.

First National City Bank of New York, using eight different nominees, appears among the top 10 of 29 utilities.

State Street Bank and Trust, Boston, using eight different nominees, appears among the top 10 of 21 utilities.

Bankers Trust of New York, using eight nominees, is among the top 10 stockholders of 20 utilities.

The other banks listed among the top 10 stockholders of 10 or more utilities are New England Merchants National Bank, Bank of New York, Northwestern National Bank of Minneapolis, United States Trust of New York, Continental Illinois National Bank and Trust of Chicago, Girard Trust of Philadelphia, National Shawmut Bank of Boston, and Chemical Bank of New York.

The evidential relationships between oil companies, the banks, and gas and electric utilities is a compelling one. Whether or not collusion takes place, the opportunity and the mechanism are in place to make it possible. One again, the Clayton Act was designed to prevent the acquisition of monopoly power, not merely its abuse. Surely there is something in this cozy relationship which bears investigation.

Oil foundations and the oil industry.—Some of the largest foundations in the country have been established with oil money. A foundation can be both a means of retaining control and seeking favorable tax treatment.

Of the first 30 largest foundations in the United States in asset rank, seven have major holdings in oil company stocks and are

---

[27] Corporate Secrecy, Congressional Record, June 28, 1972.

associated with oil company founders. The three largest in terms of the market value of assets are the Rockefeller Foundation with $831 million, the Mellon Foundation with some $668 million and the Pew Memorial Trust with $367 million in 1971 (Table 28).

An examination of these foundation assets reveals a known truth—that the Rockefeller and Mellon families are the sources of great wealth deriving from the oil industry. If the assets of the

Table 28. Foundations with Assets of $100 Million or More with Large Oil Stock Portfolios, Dec. 31, 1971 (Listed in Order of Size of Total Assets)

	Year of establishment	Market Value of Assets
Rockefeller Foundation........................	1913	$830,569,000
Marathon Oil.................................		14,326,000
Mobil Oil....................................		32,775,000
Exxon.......................................		221,250,000
Standard of Indiana.........................		83,400,000
Mellon (Andrew W.) Foundation...............	1940	668,095,000
Gulf Oil Corp..............................		294,193,000
Mellon National Bank[2].....................		24,291,000
Pew Memorial Trust..........................	1948	367,435,000
Sun Oil Co.................................		264,269,000
Minerals Development Co.[1].................		101,756,000
Rockefeller Bros. Fund......................	1940	213,493,000
Exxon.......................................		29,001,000
Mobil.......................................		18,427,000
Standard of Calif..........................		8,944,000
Mellon (Richard King) Foundation............	1947	208,810,000
Gulf Oil Corp..............................		64,976,000
Commonwealth Fund..........................	1918	132,062,000
Mobil Oil..................................		15,188,000
Exxon.......................................		11,125,000
Standard of Calif..........................		9,038,000
Standard of Indiana........................		1,393,000
an Additional $4.3 million in debentures of 5 oil cos. not shown.		
Scaife (Sarah Mellon) Foundation............	1941	103,088,000
Gulf Oil Corp..............................		77,842,000

[1] A holding company for General Crude Oil stock.
[2] The bank in 1967 had 17% of Gulf Oil Corp. stock, managed 10 employee benefit funds of Gulf Oil Corp. and had four interlocking directors.
Source: Annual Reports of Foundations, 1971.

Rockefeller Foundation and the Rockefeller Brothers Fund are added together they total approximately $1 billion. Similarly, if the assets of the Andrew Mellon Foundation, the Richard King Mellon Foundation, and the Scaife (Sarah Mellon) Foundation are combined, they too total in the neighborhood of $1 billion.

Under the Tax Reform Act of 1969, a foundation is prohibited from voting in any taxable year more than half of the voting stock it purchases after May 26, 1969. Since most of the foundations with heavy oil industry holdings had acquired their stock prior to that date, it is apparent that their head start gives them the opportunity to use their voting privileges in a manner best calculated to perpetuate management control. On the other hand, the law requires foundations to reduce their holdings in a single stock to no more than 20% of the company's capital stock and the oil foundations have a number of years in which to reach this objective.

Chairman Wright Patman of the House Banking and Currency Committee introduced a bill in March 1973 intended to force foundations to give up their ability to control any single corporation. Under his measure, foundations would have 5 years to diversify so that no more than 10 percent of their assets were invested in the stock of any corporation. Its main purposes are to prevent the exercise of control of large corporations by small groups and also to safeguard beneficiaries of the foundations in the event the large single holding depreciates in value.

A possible loophole of the Act's intention may result in the fragmentation of major foundations into smaller units, each satisfying the law's requirements but cumulatively retaining sufficient strength to exercise a measure of control. The proposed 1973 Act, however, would make such efforts immeasurably more difficult.

Insurance companies and the oil industry.—Nineteen of the largest insurance companies in the United States, seeking ways to invest their money in corporate enterprise, committed a large portion of their funds to common stocks of the oil industry. Table 29, shows that these 19 companies held upwards of $5.6 billion of marketable value of oil company common stocks. The Prudential Insurance Company alone held $1.6 billion of this grand total. Other insurance companies with over a half billion dollars in oil company stocks were Equitable Life, John Hancock and Metropolitan Life.

Table 29. Investment of Insurance Companies in the Stock of Oil Companies, December 1971

Insurance Company	Oil Director Interlocks	OIL COMMON STOCK		OIL PREFERRED STOCK	
		Market Value (Millions)	Percent of Insurance Company Portfolio in Oil Common Stocks	Market Value (Millions)	Percent of Insurance Company Portfolio in Oil Preferred Stocks
Aetna		$ 61.0	7.5%	$ 32.3	0.9%
Bankers Life		127.5	0.5	16.3	3.4
Conn. Gen'l Life		140.8	N.A.	8.4	31.9
Conn. Mutual Life	Shell	218.6	1.5	57.2	9.0
Equitable Life	Continental	566.5	10.0	N.A.	N.A.
John Hancock	Commonwealth	557.7	7.1	51.2	3.8
Lincoln Nat'l	Eastern Gas	159.6	6.6	149.7	2.1
Mass. Mutual		N.A.	N.A.	44.7	7.7
Metropolitan Life	Mobil	560.6	9.2	121.7	1.5
Mutual Benefit	Amerada Hess	85.8	7.4	31.2	0.9
Mutual Life Ins.	Texaco, Cities Service	259.9	3.6	97.7	9.5
Nat'l Life		83.2	3.0	15.6	4.0
New England Mutual		157.8	9.1	58.7	1.4
New York Life	Amerada Hess, Marathon	404.3	14.3	202.7	N.A.
Northwestern Mutual	Universal Oil Prod.	376.4	6.2	181.6	1.6
Penn Mutual	Atlantic Richfield	61.4	11.7	N.A.	N.A.
Prudential	Socal, Exxon	1,643.1	10.0	88.9	8.4
Travelers		104.7	1.8	22.1	N.A.
Western & So. Life		38.7	N.A.	N.A.	N.A.

Source: Stockholdings from Reports to the D.C. Insurance Department. Director Interlocks from Chapter VI of this study.

Another indication of the importance of these holdings is the percentage that these oil company stocks represent of the total company portfolio. For the Prudential, New York Life, Equitable Life and Penn Mutual companies, their holdings of common stock in oil companies represent at least 10% of their total common stock portfolio. Other companies in which this percentage exceeds 7% are Aetna, John Hancock, Metropolitan Life, Mutual Benefit and New England Mutual.

These same 19 companies also have a stake in the preferred stock of oil companies. Together their total holdings amount to at least $1.2 billion. For both common and preferred stock, therefore, these 19 companies had a $6.8 billion concern about what happens to the oil industry.

Evidence of this concern is reflected in the overlapping directorships between insurance companies and the oil industry (Table 29). Whether or not the overlaps exist, however, is moot. The significant fact is that any institution with the voting power represented by such holdings can be a powerful friend or enemy to oil company management. These holdings, in conjunction with other institutional portfolios where overlaps exist, have the potential for considerable collusive behavior.

Oil Companies and Managing Underwriters

The oil industry has a rapacious need for capital. Even though companies' internal operations generate a large amount of cash, the fact is that they have had to turn to investment bankers to raise the billions of dollars which they need to carry on successfully their domestic and worldwide operations.

Financial institutions that assemble and represent a group of partners in bidding for a company financing are called managing underwriters. Because of their size, connections and historical relationships, they are able to mobilize the financial community in an outpouring of money on a kingly scale. A handful of prestigious firms have been recognized as leaders in these undertakings and their very names attached to an underwriting seemingly insures success of that effort. It is not unusual for one or two managing underwriters to mobilize a consortium of dozens, if not hundreds, of other banking houses, institutions, and investors to provide the needed capital for their clients.

A financial truism among these managing underwriters is the connections which they have with other financial institutions. For example, Morgan Stanley, a managing under.riter, is part of the huge holding combine of J. P. Morgan & Company. J. P. Morgan & Company controls the Morgan Guarranty Trust Company, which had the largest total of trust assets (in 1967) in the U.S. and probably in the world. Morgan Guaranty Trust, with its $17 billion of trust funds,[28] provides substantial sums of money to the oil industry, manages employee benefit funds of the respective companies and through its trust accounts, controls or influences a number of the major oil companies.

Because of their services to the oil industry and because of their pervasive influence among the general economy, investment houses are in a position to promote mergers or sales of companies.

Similarly, they can act as a binding force for joint ventures or joint bidding, which might not otherwise take place but which would be fostered by the influential position of managing underwriters with the one or more companies involved.

Ties between managing underwriters and other corporations may unduly restrict the sources of credit available to competing businesses who do not have the same links with managing underwriters that are enjoyed by a handful of oil company behemoths. This is a form of restraint on competition.

If a company has an historical link with a single underwriter, may that not also be a potential restraint of competition?

Alliances which manifest themselves in ways other than through complete or partial control are based on banking and underwriting relationships which do not result in formal interlocks. One traditional way in which bankers or managing underwriters can watch the interest of investors who look to them for guidance is to be represented in the management or board of directors of the concern for which they have issued loans. But most importantly, this alliance can also be an informal relationship based on advice and personal conference. There is not much risk in the assumption that where a banking relationship exists between an oil company and a managing underwriter over the years to the virtual exclusion of other underwriters, that a close working relationship and understanding exists

[28] The Patman, Volume I, p. 35.

regardless of the degree of interlocking directors or more formal relationships.

A $9 Billion Relationship

Between 1945 and 1972, a minimum of $9.3 billion was raised by managing underwriters and their consortiums for the oil industry.[29] This is exclusive of short-term loans which the oil industry makes to carry on its day to day operations, which have a relatively current due date, and do not become part of the funded indebtedness of the corporation.

Two-thirds of the postwar underwriting of the 30 largest oil companies has been concentrated in consortiums controlled by four managing underwriters. These four are Morgan Stanley, the First Boston Corporation, Dillon Reed and Blyth Eastman Dillon.

Even these four do not fully reveal the extent of concentration within this aspect of banking activity. Morgan Stanley alone was responsible for 40 percent of the $9.3 billion raised since 1945. Such tremendous concentration and financial strength is rarely duplicated in American business. Reference to Table 30, reveals the detail of this concentration.

Morgan Stanley has a continuing financial relationship with all of the Standard companies, except California. It has managed consortiums which provided some $915 million to Standard of Indiana, $650 million to Exxon, and $500 million to Mobil. It may have the bulk of the business of Standard of Ohio. In addition, it is also a major capital supplier to Shell, providing some $660 million since 1961. Even Texaco, which earlier had given its business to Dillon Reed, now appears to be firmly in the Morgan Stanley corral; in two issues since 1967, the latter has raised $400 million for Texaco. Thus, Morgan Stanley has performed direct financial services for at least five of the seven largest international, integrated companies.

The second largest managing underwriter for the oil industry is the First Boston Corporation. In the last 20 years it managed consortiums which produced $1.1 billion or 12% of the total funds floated in the postwar period. It's major customer is Gulf Oil for whom it has raised $500 million over a five-year period. The Mellon interests, who control Gulf, are also on the Board of Directors of the First Boston

---

[29] Moody's Industrials, 1972

Table 30. Major Managing Underwriters for the Oil Industry, 1945-72
(In Millions of Dollars)

Morgan Stanley ($3,625)		First Boston ($1,110)		Dillon Reed ($733)		Blyth, Eastman, Dillon ($692)	
Continental	$ 300	Cities Service	$ 150	Amerada Hess	$150	Ashland	$ 88
Mobil	500	Commonwealth	20	Ashland	38	Atlantic Richfield	25
Shell	660	Diamond Shamrock	40	Texaco	150	Getty	17
Indiana	915	Eastern Gas	37	Union Oil	395	Occidental	87
Exxon	650	Marathon	145			Socal	300
Sohio	200	Phillips	200			Sun	175
Texaco	400	Sun	18				
		Gulf	500				

Note: In all instances where Morgan Stanley was concerned, its prestige and strength were sufficient for it to be the sole managing underwriter of the issues which it floated. Dillon Reed shared a single small offering of Ashland but was the major managing underwriter for Amerada Hess, Union, and Texaco (prior to 1967). Blyth and Eastman Dillon Union Securities shared their underwritings with one or more other managing underwriters. In allocating sums of joint underwriters, the following rule of the thumb was used: Where two underwriters were listed, the total underwriting was split in half; three underwriters, the split was in three equal parts; etc. While not precisely accurate, these sums were small and the errors thought to be statistically unimportant.

Source: Moody's Industrials, 1972.

Corporation. Other major customers of the First Boston Corporation include Phillips Petroleum and Cities Service. It also shared with Lehman Brothers a substantial flotation for the Marathon Oil Company.

Dillon Reed led the effort to obtain the next largest underwriting sum—$733 million or 8% of the total, for four customers. The largest by far was Union Oil Company, followed by Amerada Hess. This underwriting house managed an offering for Texaco in 1958, but apparently lost the account to Morgan Stanley.

A fourth and final company—Blyth Eastman Dillon has become a major factor in oil industry underwriting largely as a result of the merger of two smaller houses. Together, this company has provided almost $700 million to a large array of companies which include primarily Standard of California and Sun Oil.

A much smaller sum of capital was raised in Europe and in many instances these efforts were headed by a subsidiary of an American institution. Morgan Stanley's Morgan Grenfell in London, and Morgan et Cie in Paris were the primary correspondents. Lehman Brothers participated several times, both domestically and in foreign consortiums.

The concentration of underwriting activity for the oil industry demonstrates one more aspect of the close association between financial institutions and the oil industry. It also underlines the industry's heavy reliance on the Morgan interests. Perhaps the Morgans and the Rockefellers, once classified as arch rivals, have learned how to work jointly with one another.

VIII. THE OIL INDUSTRY AND ACCOUNTING SERVICES

When the same accounting firms render services to a number of companies in the same industry, they act as a binding force. They contribute in conferences and individual discussions and in their professional procedures a climate of opinion and practice within which corporate policies are formed. They carry from one corporation to another some degree or common background and temper of thought which adds a measure of unity to the corporate community.

In the accounting profession, there is a group of firms known as the "Big Eight." Together, they audit more than 80 percent of the companies listed on the New York and American stock exchanges.

The services which these companies furnish include the main functions of auditing, accounting and tax assistance. In addition, they have expanded into the fields of design of information systems and data processing, job evaluation and manpower planning, consulting, executive recruiting and pension planning.

Unlike the thousands of publicly held corporations they audit, Certified Public Accounting (CPA) firms are organized as partnerships. Data on revenues, operating costs, and other significant financial figures are not a matter of public record and traditionally have been closely guarded secrets. It is estimated that individual net billings of these companies range between $100 million and $225 million annually. Approximately two-thirds of these billings are for auditing and roughly one fifth for tax services. The remainder was generally allocated to the growing field of consultation.[30]

The Problem

The pattern of accounting services for the oil industry is concentrated in little more than a handful of firms. Seven of them audit the books of the 29 largest oil companies in the United States. Arthur Andersen & Company provides services to seven oil companies; Ernst

---

[30] Business Week Magazine, McGraw Hill, April 22, 1972

& Ernst and Price Waterhouse, five each; Arthur Young & Company and Lybrand Cooper, four each; and Haskins and Sells and Peat Marwick and Mitchell, two each (Table 31).

There are undeniable advantages in the concentration of services provided by a few accounting firms. An industry expertise is devel-

Table 31. Oil Companies and Their Accountants, 1971

	Arthur Andersen	Arthur Young	Ernst & Ernst	Haskins & Sells	Lybrand Cooper	Peat, Marwick, Mitchell & Co.	Price Waterhouse
Amerada Hess		X					
Amer. Petrofina						X	
Ashland Oil			X				
Atlantic Rich					X		
Cities Service						X	
Clark Oil			X				
Commonwealth				X			
Continental		X					
Crown Central			X				
Diamond Shamrock							X
EG&F Assoc	X						
Getty Oil	X						
Gulf Oil							X
Kerr-McGee	X						
Lubrizol					X		
Marathon			X				
Mobil Oil		X					
Occidental	X						
Parker-Hanover					X		
Phillips		X					
Shell Oil							X
St. Oil of Calif							X
St. Oil of Ind							X
St. Oil of N.J.							X
St. Oil of Ohio			X				
Sun Oil					X		
Tenneco	X						
Texaco	X						
Union Oil					X		
Universal	X						
Total	7	4	5	2	4	2	5

oped which can be carried over and applied within the industry to individual firms. There can be a uniformity of approach in which "like things look alike." This standardization provides a floor of understanding which is of considerable value to analysts who are regarding the petroleum industry. Also, by branching out into other services, the accounting firms provide a one-stop service to the oil companies which may include the array of activities mentioned above. The success of these companies is pragmatic proof of the value of their skills and resources.

Nevertheless, uniformity of approach begets habits and practices which could work to the disadvantage of the public or fall into the gray area of business morality. Servicing several oil clients (or clients in any other industry) may cast an accountant's approach into a rigid mold with consequent fear of innovation or independence in auditing concepts. The history of the accounting industry reveals how uniform approaches have worked to the disadvantage of the investing public. It required the courts to dislodge them from the concept of "generally accepted accounting principles" to one in which their primary duty was interpreted to "present fairly" the condition of their auditing firms.[31]

The question of ethics in accounting principles is also at stake when four oil companies over a nine-year period were each able to increase their assets twice as fast as retained earnings (Table 32).

Table 32. Asset Growth Compared to Retained Earnings, 1963-71

Company	Increase In Assets: 1963 to 1971	Cumulative Earnings Retained 1963-71 [1]	Ratio: Increased Assets to Retained Earnings
Gulf.....................	$4,917,000,000	$2,076,000,000	2.4
Standard Calif..........	3,968,000,000	1,945,000,000	2.0
Standard Ind...........	2,445,000,000	1,258,000,000	1.9
Texaco.................	6,411,000,000	3,197,000,000	2.0

[1] Computed by totalling annual net income for each company for 9 years, subtracting portion paid out in dividends. Average payout based on average of last 4 years as follows: Gulf, 55%; California, 48%; Indiana, 48%; Texaco, 51%. Payments on preferred stock, if any, were not included.
Source: Standard & Poor on assets, net income, and average payout.

[31] Continental Vending Decision, U.S. Court of Appeals, Judge H. J. Friendly, 1969.

Servicing a number of firms in the same industry places the accountant in the role of a management conduit from which there could follow a parallelism of action and approach. Accountants can be the conduits for financing practices. In a discussion with top management, how far removed would it be for the conversation to turn to other strategies that are practiced by companies within the same industry? "Helping with problems" implies the application of know-how acquired in one concern and transmitting it to another. Where is the fine line to be drawn between an innocent professional service and an anti-competitive practice?

Table 31 shows specifically how accounting firms with two or more oil company clients can serve as conduits. Another type of conduit, less clearly observed, is the possible relationship between so-called oil company banks and oil companies:

Ernst & Ernst

   Bank Clients: Bank of America, Western Bancorporation
   Oil Company Clients: Ashland, Clark, Crown Central
   Marathon, Sohio

Peat, Marwick, Mitchell

   Bank Client: Chase Manhattan
   Oil Company Clients: Cities Service, American Petrofina

Bank of America and Western Bancorporation, both clients of Ernst and Ernst, have interlocking directors with Standard of California and Union Oil. Chase Manhattan overlaps with Atlantic Richfield, Exxon, Standard of Indiana and Diamond Shamrock. Is a pipeline of information made available through these liaisons? The above-cited illustrations exist in equal depth among other accounting firms and their bank-oil company clients.

Possible Pitfalls

When an accounting firm provides consulting services to an oil company, such as acting as a "finder" for possible acquisitions or recommending a financial or accounting officer, what happens when the acquisition or recommended executive turns out badly? Does the accountant admit his error at the next audit or does he seek to justify his actions? And does the financial officer recommended by the accountant ever suggest that the accountant be fired? While these types of services do not bear on inter-oil company relationships, they do reflect the inherent dangers of consultant relationships between accounting firms and the oil companies they service.

Peat Marwick, Ernst & Ernst and Price Waterhouse, for example, audit a number of big banks. Is there a conflict of interest created because the accountant audits both the bank and some of its corporate borrowers? If the auditor has to offer an opinion as to the quality of the bank's loan portfolio, will he reveal inside information obtained by examining the borrower's books? The extent to which this exists between accountants and oil companies is an avenue for exploration.

Why the concentration of services among only seven prestigious firms? There are at least another eight of second echelon size who if permitted to service the oil companies would open up the area of competitive practice. These include, Alexander Grant & Company; Hurdman & Cranstoun, Penny; J. K. Lasser; Laventhol, Krekstein, Horwath & Horwath; Main Lafrentz; S. D. Leidesdorf; Elmer Fox; and Harris Kerr Forster & Company.

The whole concept of concentration of accounting services within the oil industry, and indeed for the entire business community, is a neglected area of investigation. The normal rules against concentration would seem to be applicable in this polite society of mammoth accounting firms and mammoth oil establishments.

IX. SUMMARY AND RECOMMENDATIONS

The oil industry is an extraordinarily sophisticated mechanism that has over the years developed the means to pursue a series of seemingly monopolistic practices. To do this it has marshalled a hard crust of legal precedent, at other times what may be only a patina of legality, an enormous combativeness in the courts which either enlists or cows the governmental processes, and finally a winning public relations posture. On the surface it accomplishes these practices through a series of permissible arrangements such as joint ventures, exchange agreements, control of competing energy sources, an occasional primary director interlock, industry associations, vertical integration from the mining of crude through the marketing of finished products, and other similar structural and contractual accommodations.

These surface legalities, however, are but a part of the means to achieve rationalization of action within the oil industry—the tip of the iceberg above water so to speak. Underneath there lurks a loosely knit but strongly woven fabric of intra- and inter-industry relationships which are without equal in any other industry in any part of the globe. These relationships are not reflected in a group of cigar-smoking individuals conniving in unison in a smoke-filled back room. If the latter arrangements exist, this study has no knowledge of them. Rather it is joint agreement reached by gentlemen who think alike, business leaders whose protection of and concern for one another masks an instinct for self survival, people and institutions who thrive on reciprocal favors, men of substance interested in the preservation of wealth and power, and deft operators whose very last operational techniques would be to pursue an objective frontally or with full disclosure.

Here we refer to the exquisite tapestry of the secondary director interlock, the financial institutions that nurture life in a corporate body, the trust departments of mammoth banks which exercise voting control often in secrecy, bank management of oil company pension portfolios conferred by incumbent management expecting in return to be perpetuated in office, and a second-line bulwark of insurance companies, investment trusts, and foundations all acting to preserve their hegemony by conforming to the rules of the game.

The conduits of communication which hold them together are the interlocking directorates, financial associations, the worldwide and amazingly numerous joint ventures which permit exchange of plans and actions, and the handful of accounting firms and other professionals who service the oil industry and act, perhaps unwittingly but no less effectively, as a unifying force in providing a climate of opinion and practice within which corporate policies are formed.

Through these various strategems of organization and relationships, a permanent status exists between members of the oil industry which establishes in fact, though not perhaps in legal theory, a collective behavior.

Antitrust Approach Should Attack Structure

The emphasis in this study is on the interlocking structure of the oil industry and their friendly affinities. They are the truly enduring ties because they reflect the sinews of control. Their durable relationships and dependence make joint action possible. It largely explains why this study has generally avoided the collusive practices which can and do arise from these lasting relationships. These practices against the public interest are as ingenious as the human mind can make them and as numerous as granules of grain in a silo. Banish one and another takes place. In the final analysis, however, they are only symptomatic because they do not reflect the root cause. Thus we have not talked about price fixing, actions to drive out the independent gas marketeer, efforts to influence domestic and foreign policy, restrictive selling practices and the like. When the courts find against

120

the oil industry on these symptoms, cease-and-desist orders and consent agreements are frequently only palliative. The basic approach should be to break up the control relationships which make joint action possible.

Section 7 of the Clayton Act provides the legal muscle to do just that. The whole purpose of section 7 is not whether the evils of collusion, restraint of trade or other oligopolistic actions have actually taken place. Rather it is whether the oil industry has the power to do that, whether the possibility exists for it to happen. The purpose of section 7 is to arrest anti-competitive practices in their incipiency and not after they have taken place.

It is difficult to subscribe to the reasoning which justifies oil company joint ventures on share-the-risk grounds. An oligopolistic venture obviously provides more security to the participants. A monopoly affords even more safety. But the Congress and the public have historically maintained that the evils of corporate oligopoly outweigh the financial advantages to the partners. Moreover, firms in other industries take great risks alone. Corporate development is replete with instances of gambles won and lost by major firms not nearly as affluent as the oil companies. If indeed the defense is that smaller companies do not have the financial strength to go it alone, why is it that the largest oil companies have the greatest number of participations? It would appear that the conceptual nature of our antitrust legislation points in one direction and that actual practice by the oil industry points in another.

Both the formal and informal relationships described in this study are presumably legal since they are allowed to exist. Nevertheless, many are in that gray area where changes in political philosophy, administrative aggressiveness, or consumer ground swells can alter the approach to antitrust proceedings.

From a pragmatic standpoint, the time for challenge could be ripe today. Shortage of gasoline supplies, the perplexing question of failure of the oil industry to expand its refining capacity, the suspicion of joint strategy on the trans-Alaska pipeline, foreign policy meddling, the history of oil spills and damage to the environment, and the frustration of an aroused public who somehow feels it has been taken advantage of, all lead to the possible conclusion that a suit against the oil industry might not only be welcomed but might happily prove successful.

FINDINGS

The more important findings of this study are as follows:

1. The oil industry is not only vertically integrated, but is reaching out to control competing forms of energy. They account for approximately 84% of U.S. refining capacity; about 72% of the natural gas production and reserve ownership; 30% of the domestic coal reserves and some 20% of the domestic coal production capacity; and over 50% of the uranium reserves and 25% of the uranium milling capacity.

This could result in (a) dwindling of available fuel supplies;

(b) higher prices; (c) fewer competitors; and (d) delay in substituting competing fuels through concentration of control.

2. The oil industry not only is (1) vertically integrated and (2) reaching out to control competing energy forms, but is also (3) doing the bulk of the research in liquefaction and gasification of coal. There is the danger that their experimental zeal may be tempered until they can write off their expensive refining equipment. Their research accomplishments to date have been less than satisfactory.

3. Joint ventures in the oil industry appear to be the legally sanctioned, yet not fully challenged, device that permits anti-competitive behavior on a grand scale. Cooperative relationships set up by these ventures easily number in the thousands, if not tens of thousands. They operate in every corner of the globe and are most visible in the U.S. in pipeline ownership, joint bidding, and oil and gas extraction arising out of joint bidding.

4. Director interlocks are an important means of harmonizing activities in the oil industry. While the law forbids direct interlocks between one oil company and another, the oil industry has the potential, if not the actual, means of establishing a commonality of ideas and behavior (in addition to joint ventures) through the financial community. There is a free interchange of directors between oil companies and banks; specifically, 14 banks exchanged 30 directors with 17 oil companies. The banks, through their own interlocks, harness the gas and electric utility industry, the last remaining energy producer outside the ownership orbit of the oil companies. The potential for a uniform vote or parallelism of action is largely present.

5. Relationships between the oil industry and the financial community go far beyond interlocking directorships. The potential for joint action is enhanced by the control of blocks of oil company stocks held by banks, insurance companies, investment trusts and foundations. Bank management of oil company employee benefit funds (there were 31 such funds under control of 9 banks) not only provide financial institutions the muscle to vote large blocks of stocks but by the interlocking directorates and opportunities for mutual benefit, provide the means for cozy relationships which perpetuate oil company management in power.

6. Seven accounting firms share the bulk of oil company busi-

ness. In general, they provide consulting services, executive search, data processing know-how and a raft of other services in addition to their tax and auditing specialties. The potential for anti-competitive practice arising out of such concentration is that these accounting firms can act as a binding force within the industry, contributing in conferences and individual discussions a uniform climate of opinion and practice within which corporate policies are formed. They add a measure of unity to the oil corporate community.

7. There is some suspicion that the cry of "energy shortage" may be inspired as a means of achieving higher prices. Oil companies have defied the government by refusing to reveal their gas reserve figures upon which they are predicating gas shortage. While there may be a stringency in domestic crude oil supplies, there does not appear to be a worldwide shortage and relaxation of import quotas should ease the situation. It is now belatedly revealed that lack of refining capacity is one of the major bottlenecks in the current gasoline shortage. Why is it that virtually the entire industry, with the finest economists money can buy, made the same error in not foreseeing the expansion in gasoline consumption and coming to grips with the refinery problems? Oil company acquisitions of competing energy companies opens up the possibility of supply manipulation for the petroleum industry's profit advantage; a Congressional committee alleges that one oil company may be limiting inter-fuel competition by its too-slow development of coal reserves. Moreover, experimentation in converting coal to gas and oil, concentrated in the oil industry and affiliated groups, has not been proceeding as well as might be expected, raising the possibility of less than aggressive research efforts.

RECOMMENDATIONS

Acquisition of Competing Energy Sources

1. The government should initiate antitrust proceeding against oil companies who have acquired competing energy sources such as coal, uranium, oil shale, and tar sands. The Continental Oil-Consolidation Coal merger decision should be reopened as part of these proceedings.

2. Whether as part of such antitrust proceeding or separately,

a study should be undertaken of the possible existence of a parallelism of action within the energy industries and the role played by finanical institutions. The avenues of investigation should include, although not be confined to, choices by utilities of fuel in relation to price and other factors, choice of fuel supplier in relation to director interlocks, alacrity of utilities to pass along price increases as a substitute to an analysis of fuel substitutability, similarities in advocacy of policy by oil companies and financial institutions, and comparative price increases among energy suppliers.

Natural Gas Reserves

3. Estimated gas reserves in the U.S. is an important component of pricing, national energy policy, tanker subsidies, etc. The government should make independent periodic surveys of natural gas reserves instead of relying on an industry-wide figure submitted by the American Gas Association. Its immediate purposes should assess whether the industry has underestimated these reserves and whether they colluded in so doing.

Pricing

4. The oil and natural gas industry advances the thesis that it needs more incentive to explore for these fuels. In view of previous increases granted the natural gas industry in 1968 and 1971, the Government should assess the impact of higher prices on exploration and production.

5. In a regulated industry such as natural gas, why should costs of alternative fuels be permitted to determine the price of gas when it costs far less to produce? The increase granted should be related to costs and a fair profit and only continued regulation, not deregulation, can assure that the consumer will not be gouged.

6. The Federal Power Commission should require individual company cost and profit data rather than accepting an industry-wide figure in rate increase cases. These detailed data would enable the FPC to make a better assessment of such pleas.

7. Oil companies should not be permitted to make requests for rate increases based on a single product of their operations. Rather, the overall product return should be the yardstick for price adjustments which would hopefully curtail opportunities for accounting and financial juggling of company figures.

8. A crash research program is needed in the gasification and liquefaction of coal. Additional efforts should be directed to making high-sulphur coal less toxic to the environment. Government appropriations should be expanded sharply to accelerate the research program.

9. Research awards should go in greater and more substantive amounts to companies outside the domination of the oil industry.

10. The government itself should be given a greater role in the experimentation, perhaps through the creation of a TVA-like authority, or National Bureau of Standards participation. Not only would this enhance the research effort but it would provide a cost yardstick for the benefit of consumers.

Joint Ventures

11. The legality of joint ventures should be vigorously tested in the courts. Two approaches that might be used are the concentration of economic power of the parents and the "conscious parallelism of action" doctrine.

12. The formation of joint ventures by two or more partners in the same industry or in different industries should derive their legality from the market shares of each parent in the stipulated geographical area.

13. Joint ventures should not be allowed to continue indefinitely. Time limitations should be fixed after which the joint venture may be set up as a separate company, sold to another owner, or purchased by one of the parents.

14. The scope of the present FTC prior notification regulation for mergers should be extended to include the formation of new joint ventures.

15. The SEC should require joint ventures to be listed in company reporting regardless of the size-of-share ownership. At present such ownership is required to be shown only if the share is 50% or more. The reporting should also include joint bids which culminate in joint ventures, exchange agreements, terminal facilities, and other joint arrangements.

16. The ICC should take a larger regulatory role in pipelines, many of which are joint ventures, and should be given the power to approve the building of pipelines as well as their abandonment.

17. Joint ventures, to alleviate their anti-competitive effects, should make all their patents and know-how available to any applicant on nondiscriminatory terms.

Interlocking Directorates

18. The Department of Justice and/or the Federal Trade Commission should move vigorously against director overlaps between the oil industry and other independent energy companies.

19. Congress should not tolerate interlocking in the second degree that it has made unlawful in the first degree. Overlapping between banks and oil companies, oil companies and foundations, banks and public utilities, and banks with other financial institutions provide the opportunity for joint action and entrenched privilege which strikes at the heart of our democratic institutions.

The Oil Industry and Financial Institutions

20. Corporate ownership should be stripped of secrecy. Nominee accounts, "street names", and such other devices whose purpose it is to conceal ownership should be made unlawful. A corporate ownership report act should require identity of proprietary owners of significant amounts of stock and the definition of "significance" should be considerably less than 10%.

21. Regularized detailed reporting of portfolio holdings by bank trust departments, pension funds and other institutional investors, how they voted these stocks, and what they bought and sold should be made a legal requirement.

22. Control of financial institutions over American (and the energy) industries should be diluted. Limitations should be applied on the amount of stock which institutions are permitted to hold in a single corporation. Banks should not be permitted to vote stock in employee benefit accounts which they manage. Sole voting discretion of trust accounts should be abolished, shifting back to the proprietary owners the responsibility for corporate voting.

23. Support should be given the proposed act by Representative Patman limiting investment of foundations to no more than 10% of their assets in the stock of a single corporation. In so doing, foundations should not be permitted to fragment themselves so that they may accumulate their smaller ownerships into a larger one.

24. Dominance of the capital market for the oil industry by one or two managing underwriters should be investigated and antitrust action taken if appropriate.

Accounting Serviecs to the Oil Industry

25. The SEC should require integrated oil companies to file economic and finanical reports separately for their four levels of operation (producing, transmission, refining and marketing) at home and abroad.

26. The principles which govern oil industry accounting need examination. Areas for investigation are the manner in which profits are handled between production transmission refining and marketing, how foreign earnings are treated, how assets are valued, safe guards in distinguishing between "new" and old gas discoveries, subsidiary and joint venture consolidations, etc.

27. Concentration of accounting services for the oil industry in a handful of firms may lead to abuses which are not in the public interest. A limitation on the number of clients such firms can service in a single industry, or a limitation on servicing clients such as oil companies and banks where such overlapping service may create a conflict of interest, should be imposed on the accounting profession.

Market Share Concept

28. A redefinition of the market share concept may be in order: (a) prohibitions should be on a regional as well as on a national basis for all levels of the oil industry; and (b) the mathematical formula approach (i.e. 20% of the market, the four largest, etc.) may not be appropriate if companies are tied to one another through banking associations, interlocking directors, joint ventures, and family or personal relationships. Similarly, the percent of acquisition of a competing energy industry could conceal more far-reaching relationships through formal or informal combination devices.

General

29. A full-scale investigation should be undertaken by the Congress rather than by the component agencies of the government to determine the validity of the so-called energy crises and to suggest proposed courses of action.

APPENDIX

APPENDIX

APPENDIX I

Selected Joint Ventures in the Oil Industry, by Regions of the World, March 1973

Information on joint ventures was obtained from many sources The Federal Trade Commission made available its annual count of joint ventures collected from newspaper reports gathered by the Commission. It also made available the actual newspaper clippings. In listing these joint ventures, there is no assurance that each of them is still in existence let alone that the count is incomplete. The Interstate Commerce Commission provided complete data on joint ventures in U.S. pipelines and systems. Other references included industry compilations and independent studies conducted over a period of time.

AFRICA

Name	Companies Involved	Location	Description
Central African Petroleum Refineries (PVT) Ltd.	Shell, BP, Mobil Texaco, St. (Cal.), Total	Rhodesia	Refinery (20,000 barrel/day)
Conch International Methane Ltd.	Continental Shell	Algeria	Natural gas plant
Oasis Oil Co. of Libya, Ltd.	Amerada Hess, Continental, Marathon, Shell	Libya	Mining, refining, and transmission
BP & Shell Petroleum Development Co. of Kenya	BP, Shell	Kenya	N.A.
Shell & BP Petroleum Development Co. of Nigeria	BP, Shell	Nigeria	N.A.
Shell & BP South African Manufacturing	BP, Shell	South Africa	N.A.
Shell & BP South African Petroleum Refineries	BP, Shell	South Africa	Refinery
Shell & BP (Sudan)	BP, Shell	Sudan	N.A.
Societe Equatoriale de Rafinage	CFP, Mobil, Elf Union Group, Shell, Texaco, Petrofina, BP, AGIP	Gabon	Refinery (850,000 ton/year)
United Petroleum Securities Corp.	Gulf, St. Oil (N.J.)	Africa	Owns a controlling interest in a French corporation which refines and markets petroleum products in Europe and Africa
None Given	Sunray DX (Sun) Skelly, Clark	Mozambique	Oil exploration venture— 15,000,000 acres both offshore and onshore.

Name	Companies Involved	Location	Description
Australasian Petroleum Co. Proprietary Ltd.	Oil Search Ltd., BP Group, Mobil Oil	Australia	Oil exploration
Bataan Refining Corp.	Exxon, Mobil	Philippines	Refinery
BP-Shell Aquitaine & Todd Petroleum Development	BP, Shell	New Zealand	N.A.
Frome-Broken Hill Co. Pty., Ltd.	Mobil, BP Group, Interstate Oil Ltd.	Australia	Exploration and acquisition of oil and natural gas bearing properties
Island Exploration Co. Pty., Ltd.	BP, Mobil, Oil Search Ltd.	Australia	Oil exploration
Shell-BP Pipeline Services	Shell, BP	New Zealand	Pipelines
Shell, BP and Todd Oil Services, Ltd.	Shell, BP	New Zealand	N.A.
P.T. Stanvac Indonesia	Exxon, Mobil	Indonesia	Oil exploration and production
Toa Nenryo Kogyo Kabushiki Kaisha	Mobil, Exxon, Japanese firm	Japan	Refinery
West Australian Petroleum Pty., Ltd.	Standard of Calif., Texaco, Shell, Ampol Exp., Ltd.	Australia	Holds permit to search for oil over some 213,000 square miles
None Given	Standard of Calif., Texaco	Okinawa	Refinery (28,500 barrel/day)
None Given	Texaco, Standard of Calif., Mobil, Royal Dutch Shell Group, Exxon, Getty	Philippines	Lubricating oil refinery

Name	Companies Involved	Location	Description
BP-California Ltd.	Standard of Calif., BP	United Kingdom	N.A.
Consolidated Petroleum Co., Ltd.	Shell, BP	London, England	Holding company
Cyprus Petroleum Refinery Ltd.	Mobil, BP, Shell	Cyprus	Refinery (15,000 barrel/day)
Gewerkschaft Brigitta	Shell, Exxon	West Germany	Crude oil and natural gas exploration and production
Gewerkscraft Elwerath	Shell, Exxon	West Germany	Operates oil and gas producing properties
Hellenic Petroleum Refining Co.	Mobil, Shell, Hellenic Shipyards, National Bank of Greece	Greece	Refinery (40,000 barrels/day)
Irish Refining Co.	BP, Exxon, Shell, Texaco	Ireland	Refinery
Irish Shell & BP	Shell, BP	Ireland	N.A.
Nord-West Oelleitung Gmbt.	BP, Exxon, Erdol-Raffinerie Duisburg, Union Rheinische Braun-Kohln-Kraftsoff, Veba-Chemie	West Germany	Pipeline
N.V. Nederlandse Aardolie Mij. (NAM)	Shell, Exxon	Netherlands	Drilling, development, exploring and marketing of crude oil and natural gas.
N.V. Rotterdam Rijn Pijpleiding Mij.	Shell, Mobil, Standard of Calif., Texaco, Dutch firm	Netherlands	Product and crude oil pipeline between Rotterdam and Rhine Basin in Germany.

Company	Participants	Location	Description
Oberrheinishe Mineral-oelwerke Gmbtt.	Veba-Chemie, Texaco, Continental	West Germany	Refinery (140,000 barrels/day)
Raffinerie de Cressier, S.A.	Shell, Gulf	Switzerland	Refinery
Rafinerie du Sud-Quest, S.A.	BP, AGIP, Texaco, Social, Total	Austria	Production of crude oil and natural gas.
Sarpom	Exxon, Texaco Standard of Calif.	Italy	Refinery
Shell & BP Scotland, Ltd.	Shell, BP	Scotland	N.A.
Texaco Luxembourg, S.A.	Texaco, Standard of Calif.	Luxembourg	Concentrates its activities in the oil and oil derivation industry.
Transalpine Pipeline (TAL)	Exxon, Shell, BP, Mobil, Texaco, Marathon, Continental, EENI, Gelsenbrg, Veba-Chemie, Wintershall, CFP	Austria	289 miles of 40 inch pipeline serving Austria and South Germany.
United Kingdom Oil Pipeline Ltd.	Shell, BP	United Kingdom	Oil pipeline
None Given	Royal Dutch-Shell Group, Exxon, BP	Netherlands	1 billion guilder tank complex for crude oil and oil products.
None Given	Standard of Indiana, British Gas Council, Amerada Hess, Texas Eastern Transmission Corp.	North Sea	$70,000,000 natural gas development program-onshore and offshore processing facilities.
	Marathon, Continental, Envoy Oil Ltd.	England	Exploration for and production of crude oil and natural gas.

MIDDLE EAST

Name	Companies Involved	Location	Description
Anadolu Tasfiyehanesi, A.S.	Mobil, Shell, BP	Turkey	Refinery
Arabian American Oil Co.	Texaco, Exxon, Standard of Calif., Mobil	Saudi Arabia	Exploration, production, transportation and refining of oil and oil products.
ARAMCO Overseas Co.	Texaco, Exxon, Standard of Calif., Mobil	Saudi Arabia	N.A.
ARAMCO Realty Co.	Texaco, Exxon, Standard of Calif., Mobil	Saudi Arabia	N.A.
Iranian Offshore Petroleum Co.	CEP, Atlantic Richfield, Cities Service, Superior, Kerr-McGee, Sun, National Iranian Oil Co.	Iran	N.A.
Iranium Oil Consortium	BP, Shell, Gulf, Mobil, Exxon, Texaco, Standard of Calif., CFP, Am. Independent Oil Co., Atlantic	Iran	Exploration, production, transportation, and refining of oil and oil products.
Iranium Oil Consortium	Richfield, Getty, Continental, Standard of Ohio		
Iraq Petroleum Co. (IPC)	BP, Shell, CFP, Exxon, Mobil, Gulbenkian estate	Iraq	Exploration, production, transportation and refining of oil and oil products.

MIDDLE EAST (Cont'd)

Kuwait Chemical Fertilizer Co.	BP, Gulf, Petrochemical Industries Co.	Kuwait	N.A.
Kuwait Oil Co., Ltd.	Gulf, BP	Kuwait	Exploration, production, transportation and refining of oil and oil products.
Lavaan Petroleum Co.	Atlantic Richfield, Murphy Oil, Union Oil, National Iranian Oil Co.	Iran	Exploration and production of oil.
Near East Development Corp.	Mobil, Exxon	Iraq	N.A.
Quatar Petroleum Co., Ltd.	BP, Shell, CFP, Mobil, Exxon	Quatar	N.A.
Trans Arabian Pipeline Co.	Exxon, Texaco, Standard of Calif., Mobil	Saudi Arabia	Pipeline
None Given	Gulf, BP, Kuwait, government	Kuwait	Natural gas facility ($30,000,000)
	Continental, BP, Texaco, Sun	Arabian Gulf	Development of the fateh oil fields, including use of 500,00 barrel, submerged storage vessel.

SOUTH AMERICA

Name	Companies Involved	Location	Description
Columbia-Cities Service Petroleum Corp.	Cities Service, Atlantic Richfield, Standard of Ind., Ecopetrol	Columbia	N.A.
Columbian Petroleum Company	Texaco, Mobil	Columbia	N.A.
South American Gulf Oil Co.	Mobil, Texaco	Venezuela	Crude oil transporters.
Venezuela Gulf Refining Co.	Texaco, Gulf	Venezuela	N.A.
None Given	Texaco, Gulf	Ecuador	Exploration and drilling.
None Given	Sun, Atlantic Richfield, Texaco	Venezuela	Gas compression plant $45,-000,000). Handles 150,000,000 cubic ft. of gas daily
None Given	Sun, Atlantic Richfield, Texaco, Venezuela Petrochemical Institute	Venezuela	Ammonia plant with capacity of 1,500 ton/day.
None Given	Sun, Texaco, Phillips, Shell	Venezuela	Natural gas liquids plant with a capacity of 26,000 bbls daily.

NORTH AMERICA

Name	Companies Involved	Location	Description
Oil Insurance Ltd.	Atlantic Richfield, Gulf Cities Service, Signal, Standard Oil of Calif., Phillips, Union, Marathon	North America	To insure its members' onshore, offshore property against liability involving pollution.
Pipelines of Puerto Rico, Inc.	Shell, Texaco, Commonwealth	Puerto Rico	Products pipeline
Raffinerie des Antilles, S.A.	Elf Union, CFP, Shell, Exxon, Texaco	Martinique	Refinerie (550,000 ton/year)
Refineria Petrolera Acajutla, S.A.	Shell, Exxon	El Salvador	Refinery (14,000 barrels/day)
Refineria Petrolera de Guatemala-California Inc.	Standard of Calif., Shell	Guatemala	Refinery (12,000 barrels/day)
Shell-Mex and BP, Ltd.	Shell, BP	Mexico	N.A.
Standard Oil Co. of Ohio	BP, Standard of Ohio	Ohio	BP owns nearly a 50% interest in Standard of Ohio.
Syncrude Canada	Atlantic Richfield, Exxon, Cities Service, Gulf	Canada	Extraction of crude oil from the Athabasco oil sands.
THUMS Long Beach Co.	Texaco, Union, Exxon, Mobil, Shell	California	Developing oil field off Long Beach.

NORTH AMERICA (Cont'd)

None Given	Texaco, Standard of Ind., Exxon, Argonaut, Ashland, Perry, R. Bass, Dixilyn, Hamilton Bros., Occidental, Offshore Co., Pennzoil United, Shell, Tenneco, Texas Production, Trans-Ocean Oil, Gulf, Midwest Oil	Louisiana	Proposed joint gas processing plant.
None Given	Standard of Ohio, Mobil, Standard of Ind., Texas Pacific Oil Co.	Oklahoma	Oil recovery project ($10,000,000)
None Given	Standard of Ind., Phillips, Atlantic Richfield, Skelly	Alaska	Completion of a well that produced 1,500 barrels a day, plus 11 other exploratory wells.
None Given	Sun, Superior, Marathon Texaco, Standard of California	California	Offshore drilling (see footnote)
Caltex[1]		Worldwide	

[1] Texaco and Standard Oil of California are involved in a worldwide joint venture, Caltex, which consists primarily of four companies: American Overseas Petroleum Ltd., Caltex Petroleum Corp., Caltex Trading Company, Inc., and P.T. Caltex Pacific Indonesia. Ownership in these companies is divided evenly between Texaco and Standard Oil of California. Caltex operates in over 40 countries throughout the world. It would be difficult to determine a number which would reflect the extent of the joint involvement in the Caltex group of companies. Therefore, the Caltex group has been counted as *one* joint venture, and only one working relationship between Texaco and Standard of California. Thus, the N.A. Continental joint venture tables as well as the summary table considerably understate the bonds of cooperation which tie these two oil companies together.

OIL AND OTHER INDUSTRIES

Name	Companies Involved	Location	Description
C-A Nuclear Fuels	Aerojet, General, Continental	California	Full scale nuclear fuel bundles would be designed, fabricated, and tested for qualification.
Conquista	Continental, Pioneer Natural Gas Co.	Texas	Uranium mining and milling project.
Dillingham Petroleum Corp.	Dillingham Corp., Continental	Hawaii	Build a $60 million oil refinery with a capacity of 50,000 barrels a day.
Gulf United Nuclear Fuels Corp.	Gulf, United Nuclear Corp.	U.S.	To design, manufacture, and sell nuclear fuel for light-water nuclear power reactors.
Realty Growth Investors	Gulf, Equitable Trust Co.	Maryland	Private real estate venture.
Rocky Mountain Associated Coal Corp.	Eastern Gas & Fuel Associates, Union Pacific Corp.	Wyoming	To mine low-sulphur coal for sale in domestic and foreign markets.
None Given	Jones & Laughlin Steel Corp., Diamond Shamrock	W. Virginia	Coal mine and preparation plant.
None Given	Allied Chemical, Gulf	South Carolina	To process used nuclear fuel from atomic power plant.

OIL AND OTHER INDUSTRIES (Cont'd)

Company	Location	Purpose	Amount
Freeport Minerals, Brewster Phosphates, Kerr-McGee Corp.	Louisiana	To process phosphate rock into phosphoric acid.	None Given
Commonwealth, PPG Industries	Puerto Rico	Large olefins plant	None Given
Commonwealth, W. R. Grace & Co.	Puerto Rico	Oxo-alcohol plant	None Given
Gulf, Pan American World Airways, Inc.	Europe	To build and operate motels	None Given
Shell, Union Pacific Railroad	Colorado	Exploration for oil	None Given
Holiday Inns Towers International, Occidental	Eastern Europe	To build and operate motels	None Given
Marathon, Vitro Corp. of America	Rocky Mountains	Exploration for uranium	None Given
Atlantic Richfield, Denison Mines, Ltd.	Manitoba	Uranium exploration program	None Given
Union, Nuclear Reserves, Inc.	Wyoming	Uranium exploration program	None Given
Gulf, Uranerzberghau, Gulf Mineral Resources Co.	Saskatchewan	Uranium concern	None Given

U.S. OIL PIPELINE COMPANIES—JOINT VENTURES

Pipeline Company	Oil Companies Involved
Arahoe	Union, Atlantic Richfield
Badger	Cities Service, Union, Atlantic Richfield, Texaco
Black Lake	Placid Oil, Atlantic Richfield
Butte	Shell, Murphy, Continental, Burlington-Northern, Western Crude Oil
Cherokee	Gulf, Continental
Chicap	Union, Standard of Indiana, Clark
Colonial	Standard of Indiana, Atlantic Richfield, BP, Cities Service, Continental, Mobil, Phillips, Texaco, Gulf, Union
Cook Inlet	Atlantic Richfield, Marathon, Mobil, Union
Four Corners	Continental, Gulf, Atlantic Richfield, Shell, Standard of California, Superior
Jayhawk	Colombia Oil and Gas, National Cooperative Refinery Association
Kaw	Cities Service, Phillips, Texaco
Lake Charles	Cities Service, Continental
Laurel	BP, Gulf, Texaco
Mid-Valley	Sun, Standard of Ohio, Gulf
Olympic	Mobil, Shell, Texaco
Pioneer	Continental, Atlantic Richfield
Plantation	Exxon, Shell, Standard of California
Platte	Continental, Marathon, Union, Atlantic Richfield, Gulf
Portal	Hunt Oil, Burlington-Northern
Southcap	Union, Clark
Tecumseh	Atlantic Richfield, Union Ashland
Texaco-Cities Service	Texaco, Cities Service
Texas-New Mexico	Texaco, Atlantic Richfield, Cities Service, Getty
West Shore	Standard of Indiana, Shell, Mobil, Texaco, Marathon, Clark, Cities Service, Continental Union, Exxon
West Texas Gulf	Gulf, Cities Service, Sun, Union, Standard of Ohio
White Shoal	Kerr McGee, Cabot Corp., Case-Pomeroy, Felmont
Wolverine	Cities Service, Clark, Marathon, Mobil, Shell, Texaco, Union
WYCO	Standard of Indiana, Texaco, Mobil
Yellowstone	Exxon, Continental

Pipeline System	Companies Involved	Mileage
ARCO-Pure (Microwave)	Atlantic Richfield, Union	None
ATA Products	Phillips, Texaco, Diamond Shamrock	277
Basin	Texaco, Atlantic Richfield, Cities Service, Shell	348
Bayou	Atlantic Richfield, Crown, Crown Central, Marathon, Shell	252
Borger-Denver Products	Diamond Shamrock, Phillips	None
Capline	Ashland, Marathon, Sun, Gulf, Standard of Ohio, Standard of Indiana, Shell, Union, Clark, Texaco	647
Capwood	Shell, Clark	56
Casa	Atlantic Richfield, Gulf	248
Crown-Shell Baytown Feederline	Crown, Shell	14
Cushing-Chicago	Atlantic Richfield, Union	685
East Texas Mainline	Texaco, Crown Central, Cities Service	259
Harbor	Atlantic Richfield, Texaco, Gulf	95
L & L	N.A.	96
Mesa	Cities Service, Gulf, Sun, Union	150
Medicine Bow	Skelly, Plasco	205
Ozark	Shell, Texaco	443
Port Arthur	Texaco, Union, Gulf	None
Rancho	Atlantic Richfield, Ashland, Crown Central, Acorn, Phillips, Shell	461
Saal	Phillips, Texaco, Diamond Shamrock	101
Ship Shoal	Shell, Union, Hunt	68
Whitecap	Union, Hunt, Kerr McGee, Cabot Corp., Case-Pomeroy, Felmont	44
Wood River	Texaco, Marathon	54

APPENDIX II

Rationale for Deletion of Oil Company Officers Who are Not Directors

Our initial outline of proposed avenues for an anti-trust approach to the oil companies suggested a study of the overlapping directorships between these companies. In compiling the data for their study, the question arose as to whether the names of officers (who were not also directors) should be included. We concluded that the involvement of such officers in interlocks of any kind was not sufficient to warrant the inclusion of their names in the data.

The analysis which enabled us to reach this conclusion consisted of a comparison between the number of interlocks for directors and the corresponding number of officers (who were not directors). We selected six directors from each of the six largest oil companies in the United States (ranked by sales). We then checked the Standard and Poor's Corporate Register to observe if any of these men served as directors for other oil companies, financial institutions, insurance companies, or companies producing competing forms of energy. The results were as follows: Nine of the thirty-six directors' names were not listed; thirteen of the directors had no relevant outside interests; twelve of the directors held directorships in companies among the four classifications mentioned earlier. The remaining two directors each held *two* outside directorships in companies of interest to us.

We then selected six high ranking officers (who were *not* directors) from each of the six largest oil companies. A similar check of Standard and Poor's Corporate Register yielded the following results: Twenty-two of the officers' names were not listed. Fourteen of the officers had no relevant outside interests. None of them held directorships on boards of companies that were of concern to us.

The contrast between the two groups (directors and officers who are not directors), with regard to interlocks is significant. The type of interlock for which we are searching occurs frequently only among directors. We therefore concluded that the names of officers who are not also directors should be omitted, since such names would serve only to increase the volume of data without yielding any corresponding increase in its value.

Analysis of Interlocking Directorships in the Oil Industry

	Total	Not listed [1]	No Relevant Outside Interests [2]	Director in one Relevant Outside Company	Director in two Relevant Outside Companies
Directors*..........	36	9	13	12	2
Officers* (who are not directors)	36	22	14	0	0

* Six (6) randomly selected from each of the six largest oil companies.
[1] Source: Standard & Poor's Register of Corporations, Directors and Executives.
[2] Relevant outside interest is defined as involvement in another oil company, financial institution, insurance company, or company producing competing forms of energy.

APPENDIX III

Oil Companies: Primary and Secondary Director Interlocks With Financial and Energy Companies, October 1972 [1]

AMERADA HESS CORP.

(2) Banks	—Chemical Bank
(2) Insurance	—Equitable Life Assurance Soc. of the U.S.
Insurance	—Metropolitan Life Ins. Co.
(2) Insurance	—Mutual of New York
Insurance	—New York Life Ins. Co.
Coal	—United States Steel Corp.
Foundations	—Commonwealth Fund
Oil	—Mobil Oil Corp.
(2) Oil	—Standard Oil Co.—New Jersey
Oil	—Texaco Inc.
(2) Insurance	—Mutual Benefit Life Ins. Co.
Banks	—Chase Manhattan Bank
(2) Investment	—American Express Co.
(2) Utilities	—Public Service Electric & Gas Co.
(1) Insurance	—New York Life Ins. Co.
Banks	—Manufacturers Hanover Trust Co.
Banks	—Crocker National Bank
Banks	—Chemical Bank
Coal	—Burlington Northern Inc.
Coal	—Amax Coal Co.
(2) Foundations	—Rockefeller Foundation
Uranium	—Union Carbide Corp.
Utilities	—American Electric Power (NY)
(3) Utilities	—Consolidated Edison
Oil	—Marathon Oil Co.
Oil	—Shell Oil Co.
Banks	—First National City Bank
Insurance	—Conn Mutual Life Ins. Co.
(4) Oil	—Royal Dutch/Shell Group of Comps.

AMERICAN PETROFINA, INC.

Investment	—Investors Diversified Services, Inc.
(2) Coal	—Pittston Co.
Gas Pipelines	—Northern Natural Gas. Co.
Insurance	—Bankers Life Co.
Coal	—Consolidation Coal Co.

---

[1] Indented companies following each oil company represent a primary inter-lock; thus, Royal Dutch/Shell has 4 direct interlocks with Shell Oil. The other firms reflect second level overlaps; thus, Shell Oil has a primary interlock with First National City Bank, Connecticut Mutual Life Insurance and Amerada Hess.

Banks	—Chase Manhattan Bank
Banks	—First Bank System, Inc.
Banks	—First Chicago Corp.
Insurance	—Equitable Life Assurance Soc. of the U.S.
(2) Insurance	—Metropolitan Life Ins. Co.
Insurance	—Mutual Benefit Life Ins. Co.
Investment	—American Express Co.
Investment	—Jefferson-Pilot Corp.
Foundations	—Rockefeller Foundation
Foundations	—Rockefeller Brothers Fund
Oil	—Diamond Shamrock Corp.
Oil	—Standard Oil Co.—Indiana
Oil	—Standard Oil Co.—N.J.
Banks	—Morgan Guaranty Trust Co. of New York
(2) Insurance	—Aetna Life and Casualty
Insurance	—John Hancock Mutual Life Ins. Co.
Insurance	—Metropolitan Life Ins. Co.
Insurance	—Penn Mutual Life Ins. Co.
Coal	—Burlington Northern Inc.
(2) Coal	—United States Steel Corp.
(2) Investment	—INA Corporation
Investment	—Chubb Corp.
Uranium	—Union Carbide Corp.
Gas Pipelines	—Panhandle Eastern Pipeline Co.
Utilities	—Duke Power Co.
Utilities	—Niagara Mohawk Power Corp.
Oil	—Cities Service Co.
Oil	—Continental Oil Co.
Oil	—Standard Oil Co.—N.J.
Banks	—First Chicago Corp.
Banks	—First Bank System, Inc.
Banks	—Chase Manhattan Bank
Banks	—First National City Bank
Insurance	—John Hancock Mutual Life Ins. Co.
(2) Insurance	—Metropolitan Life Ins. Co.
Insurance	—Mutual Of New York
(2) Investment	—CNA Financial Corp.
(2) Utilities	—Commonwealth Edison
(2) Insurance	—Penn Mutual Life Ins. Co.
Banks	—Manufacturers Hanover Trust Co.
Banks	—Morgan Guaranty Trust Co. of N.Y.
Utilities	—Consolidated Edison
Utilities	—Philadelphia Electric Co.
Investment	—Chubb Corp.
Banks	—The First Boston Corp.
(2) Banks	—First National City Bank
Banks	—Marine Midland Bank, Inc.
Banks	—Security Pacific National Bank
Banks	—Morgan Guaranty Trust Co. of N.Y.
Insurance	—New England Mutual Life Ins. Co.

BRITISH PETROLEUM CO., LTD.

(2) Oil	—Standard Oil Co.—Ohio
(5) Coal	—Old Ben Coal Corp.
Coal	—Republic Steel Corp.
Utilities	—Detroit Edison Co.
Oil	—Diamond Shamrock Corp.

CITIES SERVICE CO.

Banks	—Manufacturers Hanover Trust Co.
Insurance	—Penn Mutual Life Ins. Co.
Insurance	—New York Life Ins. Co.
Insurance	—Prudential Ins. Co. of America
Coal	—Amax Coal Co.
Coal	—General Dynamics Corp.
Investment	—American Express Co.
Investment	—First Charter Financial Corp.
Utilities	—Consolidated Edison
Utilities	—Public Service Electric & Gas Co.
(1) Banks	—Morgan Guaranty Trust Co. of N.Y.
(2) Insurance	—Aetna Life and Casualty
Insurance	—John Hancock Mutual Life Ins. Co.
Insurance	—Metropolitan Life Ins. Co.
Insurance	—Penn Mutual Life Ins Co.
Coal	—Burlington Northern Inc.
(2) Coal	—United States Steel Corp.
Investment	—Chubb Corp.
Uranium	—Union Carbide Corp.
Gas Pipelines	—Panhandle Eastern Pipeline Co.
Utilities	—Duke Power Co.
Utilities	—Niagara Mohawk Power Co.
Oil	—Atlantic Richfield Co.
Oil	—Continental Oil Co.
Oil	—Standard Oil Co.—N.J.
(1) Insurance	—Mutual of New York
Banks	—Bankers Trust Company
Banks	—Wells Fargo Bank, Nat. Assoc.
Banks	—Western Bancorporation
Banks	—First Chicago Corp.
(2) Coal	—Union Pacific Railroad Co.
Investment	—Merrill, Lynch, Pierce, Fenner, & Smith, Inc.
Uranium	—United Nuclear Corp.
Utilities	—Consumers Power Co.
Oil	—Texaco Inc.
Gas Pipelines	—Cities Service Gas Co.
Banks	—Security Pacific National Bank

COMMONWEALTH OIL REFINING COMPANY

Banks	—The First Boston Corporation
Investment	—Chubb Corporation
Foundations	—Mellon (Richard King) Foundation
Insurance	—John Hancock Mutual Life Ins. Company
Banks	—Morgan Guaranty Trust Co. of New York
Banks	—First Chicago Corporation
Utilities	—American Electric Power (NY)
Oil	—Eastern Gas & Fuel Associates
Coal	—Amax Coal Company
Banks	—Manufacturers Hanover Trust Company
Insurance	—New York Life Insurance Company
Utilities	—El Paso Antural Gas Company
Utilities	—Middle South Utilities, Inc.
Investment	—American Express Company
Insurance	—John Hancock Mutual Life Ins. Company
Banks	—Morgan Guaranty Trust Company of New York
Banks	—First Chicago Corporation
Utilities	—American Electric Power (NY)
Oil	—Commonwealth Oil Refining Company
(4) Coal	—Eastern Associated Coal Corporation
(2) Gas Pipelines	—Algonquin Gas Transmission Company
Oil	—Texas Eastern Transmission Corporation
Gas Pipelines	—Texas Eastern Transmission Corporation

CONTINENTAL OIL CO.

Banks	—Bankers Trust Company
Insurance	—Mutual of New York
Insurance	—Prudential Ins Co. of America
Coal	—Consolidation Coal Co.
Investment	—American Express Co.
Foundations	—Commonwealth Fund
Foundations	—Rockefeller Foundation
Oil	—Mobile Oil Corp.
Banks	—Cont'ent Ill. Nat. B&T Co., Chicago
Banks	—Northwest Bancorporation
Insurance	—Aetna Life & Casualty
Coal	—Consolidation Coal Co.
Coal	—General Dynamics Corp.
(2) Utilities	—Commonwealth Edison
(2) Oil	—Standard Oil Co.—Indiana
Oil	—Universal Oil Products Co.
Oil	—Texaco Inc.
Banks	—Morgan Guaranty Trust Co. of N.Y.
(2) Insurance	—Aetna Life and Casualty
Insurance	—John Hancock Mutual Life Ins. Co.
Insurance	—Metropolitan Life Ins. Co.
Insurance	—Penn Mutual Life Ins. Co.
Coal	—Burlington Northern Inc.

CONTINENTAL OIL CO. (Cont'd)

(2) Coal	—United States Steel Corp.
(2) Investment	—INA Corporation
Investment	—Chubb Corp.
Uranium	—Union Carbide Corp.
Gas Pipelines	—Panhandle Eastern Pipeline Co.
Utilities	—Duke Power Co.
Utilities	—Niagara Mohawk Power Corp.
Oil	—Cities Service Co.
Oil	—Atlantic Richfield
Oil	—Standard Oil Co.—New Jersey
(2) Insurance	—Equitable Life Assurance Soc. of the U.S.
Banks	—Chase Manhattan Bank
Banks	—Mellon National Bank & Trust
(2) Banks	—Chemical Bank
(2) Insurance	—Equitable Life Assurance Soc. of the U.S.
Coal	—Burlington Northern Inc.
Coal	—United States Steel Corp.
(2) Foundations	—Rockefeller Foundation
Uranium	—Rio Algom Mines Ltd.
Utilities	—American Electric Power (NY)
Utilities	—Commonwealth Edison
Utilities	—Consolidated Edison
(3) Coal	—Consolidation Coal Company
Banks	Cont'ent Ill. Nat. B&T Co., Chicago
(2) Coal	—Mathais Coal Company
Uranium	—Union Carbide Corporation
Gas Pipelines	—Northern Natural Gas Company
Utilities	—American Electric Power (NY)
(1) Coal	—Mathais Coal Company
Banks	—National Bank of Detroit

DIAMOND SHAMROCK CORP.

Banks	—Chase Manhattan Bank
Banks	—First Bank System, Inc.
Banks	—First Chicago Corp.
Insurance	—Equitable Life Assurance Soc. of the U.S.
(2) Insurance	—Metropolitan Life. Ins. Co.
Insurance	—Mutual Benefit Life Ins. Co.
Investment	—American Express Co.
Investment	—Jefferson-Pilot Corp.
Foundations	—Rockefeller Foundation
Foundations	—Rockefeller Brothers Fund
Oil	—Atlantic Richfield Co.
Oil	—Standard Oil Co.—Indiana
Oil	—Standard Oil Co.—New Jersey
Banks	—Mellon National Bank & Trust
Insurance	—Equitable Life Assurance Soc. of the U.S.

DIAMOND SHAMROCK (Cont'd)

Insurance	—Metropolitan Life Ins. Co.
Insurance	—Northwestern Mutual Life Ins. Co.
Coal	—Mathais Coal Co.
(2) Coal	—United States Steel Corp.
Investment 1	—Imperial Corp. of America
Foundations	—Mellon (Andrew W) Foundation
Foundations	—Scaife (Sarah Mellon) Foundation
Foundations	—Mellon (Richard King) Foundation
(3) Oil	—Gulf Oil Corp.
Coal	—General Dynamics Corp.
Banks	—Cont'ent Ill. Nat. B&T Co., Chicago
Banks	—Manufacturers Hanover Trust Co.
Insurance	—Mass Mutual Life Ins. Co.
(2) Coal	—General Dynamics Corp.
Oil	—Standard Oil Co.—Ohio
(5) Coal	—Old Ben Coal Corp.
Coal	—Republic Steel Corp.
Utilities	—Detroit Edison Co.
(2) Oil	—British Petroleum Co., Ltd.

GETTY OIL CO.

(2) Banks	—Bank of America
Insurance	—Prudential Ins. Co. of America
Investment	—Household Finance Corp.
Utilities	—Southern Cal. Edison
Oil	—Standard Oil of California
(2) Oil	—Union Oil Co. of California
Investment	—Cit. Financial Corp.
Banks	—Dillon, Reed, & Co.. Inc.
Utilities	—Southern Cal. Edison
Banks	—Bank of America
(3) Banks	—Western Bancorporation

GULF OIL CORP.

(3) Banks	—Mellon National Bank & Trust
Insurance	—Equitable Life Assurance Soc. of the U.S.
Insurance	—Metropolitan Life Ins. Co.
Insurance	—Northwestern Mutual Life Ins. Co.
Coal	—Mathais Coal Co.
(2) Coal	—United States Steel Corp.
Investment	—Imperial Corp. of America
Foundations	—Mellon (Andrew W) Foundation
Foundations	—Scaife (Sarah Mellon) Foundation

GULF OIL CORP. (Cont'd)

Foundations	—Mellon (Richard King) Foundation
Oil	—Diamond Shamrock Corp.
Coal	—Pittsburgh & Midland Coal Mining Co.
Foundations	—Mellon (Richard King) Foundation
Banks	—The First Boston Corp.
Banks	—Mellon National Bank & Trust
Foundations	—Scaife (Sarah Mellon) Foundation

KERR-McGEE CORP.

Banks	—Security Pacific National Bank
Coal	—Union Pacific Railroad Co.
Investment	—Chubb Corp.
Gas Pipelines	—Cities Service Gas Co.
(3) Utilities	—Southern Cal. Edison

MARATHON OIL CO.

Insurance	—New York Life Ins. Co.
Banks	—Manufacturers Hanover Trust Co.
Banks	—Crocker National Bank
Banks	—Chemical Bank
Coal	—Burlington Northern Inc.
Coal	—Amax Coal Co.
(2) Foundations	—Rockefeller Foundation
Uranium	—Union Carbide Corp.
Utilities	—American Electric Power (NY)
Utilities	—Commonwealth Edison
(3) Utilities	—Consolidated Edison
Oil	—Amerada Hess Corp.
Coal	—Republic Steel Corp.
Insurance	—Metropolitan Life Ins. Co.
Insurance	—Northwestern Mutual Life Ins. Co.
Coal	—Old Ben Coal Corp.
Gas Pipelines	—Consolidated Natural Gas Co.
Oil	—Standard Oil Co.
Uranium	—Anaconda Co.
Banks	—First Bank System, Inc.
Insurance	—Metropolitan Life Ins. Co.
Foundations	—Rockefeller Foundation

153

MOBIL OIL CORP.

	Banks	—Bankers Trust Co.
	Insurance	—Mutual of New York
	Insurance	—Prudential Ins. Co. of America
	Coal	—Consolidation Coal Co.
	Investment	—American Express Co.
	Foundations	—Commonwealth Fund
	Foundations	—Rockefeller Foundation
	Oil	—Continental Oil Co.
	Banks	—First National City Bank
	Banks	—First Chicago Corp.
	Insurance	—Metropolitan Life Ins. Co.
	Insurance	—New England Mutual Life Ins. Co.
	Insurance	—Teachers Ins. & Annuity Assn. of America
	Insurance	—Prudential Ins. Co. of America
(2)	Investment	—Chubb Corp.
	Foundations	—Rockefeller Foundation
	Utilities	—Consolidated Edison
	Oil	—Phillips Petroleum Co.
	Oil	—Shell Oil Co.
	Banks	—Chemical Bank
(2)	Insurance	—Equitable Life Assurance Soc. of the U.S.
	Insurance	—Metropolitan Life Ins. Co.
(2)	Insurance	—Mutual of New York
	Insurance	—New York Life Ins. Co.
	Coal	—Burlington Northern Inc.
	Coal	—United States Steel Corp.
	Foundations	—Commonwealth Fund
(2)	Oil	—Amerada Hess Corp.
(2)	Oil	—Standard Oil Co.—New Jersey
	Oil	—Texaco Inc.
	Insurance	—Metropolitan Life Ins. Co.
(2)	Banks	—Chase Manhattan Bank
	Banks	—First National City Bank
	Banks	—Charter New York Corp.
	Banks	—Mellon National Bank & Trust
	Banks	—Chemical Bank
	Banks	—Morgan Guaranty Trust Co. of New York
(2)	Banks	—First Chicago Corp.
	Coal	—Utah International Inc.
	Coal	—Republic Steel Corp.
	Investment	—American Express Co.
	Uranium	—Anaconda Co.
	Uranium	—Union Carbide Corp.
	Utilities	—Consolidated Edison
	Utilities	—Pacific Gas & Electric
	Investment	—Transamerica Financial Corp.
	Gas Pipelines	—Texas Eastern Transmission Corp.
	Investment	—American Express Co.
	Banks	—Bankers Trust Company
	Banks	—Manufacturers Hanover Trust Co.

154

MOBIL OIL CORP. (Cont'd)

	Banks	—Chase Manhattan Bank
	Insurance	—Conn. General Life Ins. Co.
	Insurance	—Metropolitan Life Ins. Co.
(2)	Insurance	—Mutual Benefit Life Ins. Co.
	Foundations	—Rockefeller Foundation
	Gas Pipelines	—Colorado Interstate Gas Co.
	Utilities	—Middle South Utilities, Inc.
	Utilities	—Consolidated Edison
	Banks	—Manufacturers Hanover Trust Co.
	Banks	—First National City Bank
	Insurance	—Equitable Life Assurance Soc. of the U.S.
	Insurance	—Metropolitan Life Ins. Co.
	Insurance	—Penn Mutual Life Ins. Co.
(3)	Insurance	—New York Life Ins. Co.
	Foundations	—Commonwealth Fund

OCCIDENTAL PETROLEUM CORP.

(4) Coal   —Island Creek Coal Co.

PARKER-HANNIFIN CORP.

Investment   —Financial Federation, Inc.

PHILLIPS PETROLEUM CO.

	Banks	—First National City Bank
(1)	Banks	—First Chicago Corp.
	Insurance	—Metropolitan Life Ins. Co.
	Insurance	—New England Mutual Life Ins. Co.
	Insurance	—Prudential Ins. Co. Of America
(2)	Investment	—Chubb Corp.
	Foundations	—Rockefeller Foundation
	Utilities	—Consolidated Edison
	Oil	—Mobil Oil Corp.
	Oil	—Shell Oil Co.
	Oil Pipelines	—Colonial Pipeline Co.
	Oil Pipelines	—Amoco Pipeline Co.
	Oil Pipelines	—Continental Pipeline Co.
	Oil Pipelines	—Mid-Valley Pipeline Co.

ROYAL DUTCH/SHELL GROUP OF COMPANIES

(4)	Oil	—Shell Oil Co.
	Banks	—First National City Bank
	Insurance	—Connecticut Mutual Ins. Co.
	Oil	—Amerada Hess Corp. (overlapping directorship terminated)

155

SHELL OIL COMPANY

Banks	—First National City Bank
Banks	—First Chicago Corp.
Insurance	—Metropolitan Life Ins. Co.
Insurance	—New England Mutual Life Ins. Co.
Insurance	—Teachers Ins. & Annuity Assn. of America
Insurance	—Prudential Ins. Co. of America
(2) Investment	—Chubb Corp.
Foundations	—Rockefeller Foundation
Utilities	—Consolidated Edison
Oil	—Phillips Petroleum Co.
Oil	—Mobil Oil Corp.
Insurance	—Connecticut Mutual Life Ins. Co.
(4) Oil	—Royal Dutch/Shell Group of Comps.
Oil	—America Hess Corp. (overlapping directorship terminated)
(2) Banks	—Chemical Bank
(2) Insurance	—Mutual Benefit Life Ins. Co.
Insurance	—New York Life Ins. Co.

THE SIGNAL COMPANIES, INC.

Investment	—CNA Financial Corp.
(2) Banks	—First Chicago Corp.
Coal	—Zeigler Coal Co.
Gas Pipelines	—Natural Gas Pipeline Co. of America

STANDARD OIL OF CALIFORNIA

Banks	—Bank of America
Insurance	—Prudential Ins. Co. of America
Investment	—Household Finance Corp.
Utilities	—Southern Cal. Edison
(2) Oil	—Getty Oil Co.
(2) Oil	—Union Oil Co. of California
Banks	—Crocker National Bank
Insurance	—New York Life Ins. Co.
Utilities	—Pacific Gas & Electric
(2) Banks	—Western Bancorporation
Insurance	—Mutual of New York
Utilities	—Pacific Gas & Electric
(3) Utilities	—Southern Cal Edison
Utilities	—El Paso Antural Gas Co.
Oil	—Union Oil Co. of California
Insurance	—Prudential Ins. Co. Of America
Banks	—Bankers Trust Company
Banks	—Manufacturers Hanover Trust Co.
Banks	—First National City Bank
Utilities	—Public Service Electric & Gas Co.
Oil	—Standard Oil Co.—New Jersey

STANDARD OIL COMPANY—INDIANA

(2) Banks	—Cont'ent Ill. Nat. B&T Co., Chicago
Banks	—Northwest Bancorporation
Insurance	—Aetna Life & Casualty
Coal	—Consolidation Coal Co.
Coal	—General Dynamics Corp.
(2) Utilities	—Commonwealth Edison
Oil	—Continental Oil Co.
Oil	—Universal Oil Products Co.
Oil	—Texaco Inc.
Banks	—Chase Manhattan Bank
Banks	—First Bank System, Inc.
Banks	—First Chicago Corp.
Insurance	—Equitable Life Assurance Soc. of the U.S.
(2) Insurance	—Metropolitan Life Ins. Co.
Insurance	—Mutual Benefit Life Ins. Co.
Investment	—American Express Co.
Investment	—Jefferson-Pilot Corp.
Foundations	—Rockefeller Foundation
Foundations	—Rockefeller Brothers Fund
Oil	—Atlantic Richfield Co.
Oil	—Diamond Shamrock Corp.
Oil	—Standard Oil Co.—New Jersey
Investment	—Household Finance Corp.
Banks	—Bank of America
Utilities	—Commonwealth Edison
(2) Banks	—First Chicago Corp.
Insurance	—Equitable Life Assurance Soc. of the U.S.
Insurance	—New York Life Ins. Co.

STANDARD OIL COMPANY—NEW JERSEY

Banks	—Chase Manhatan Bank
Banks	—First Bank System, Inc.
Banks	—First Chicago Corp.
Insurance	—Equitable Life Assurance Soc. of the U.S.
(2) Insurance	—Metropolitan Life Ins. Co.
Insurance	—Mutual Benefit Life Ins. Co.
Investment	—American Express Co.
Investment	—Jefferson-Pilot Corp.
Foundations	—Rockefeller Foundation
Foundations	—Rockefeller Brothers Fund
Oil	—Atlantic Richfield Co.
Oil	—Diamond Shamrock Corp.
Oil	—Standard Oil Co.—Indiana
(2) Banks	—Chemical Bank
(2) Insurance	—Equitable Life Assurance Soc. of the U.S.
Insurance	—Metropolitan Life Ins. Co.
(2) Insurance	—Mutual of New York
Insurance	—New York Life Ins. Co.

157

	Coal	—Burlington Northern Inc.
	Coal	—United States Steel Corp.
	Foundations	—Commonwealth Fund
(2)	Oil	—Amerada Hess Corp.
	Oil	—Mobile Oil Corp.
	Oil	—Texaco Inc.
	Banks	—Morgan Guaranty Trust Co. of N.Y.
(2)	Insurance	—Aetna Life & Casualty
	Insurance	—John Hancock Mutual Life Ins. Co.
(2)	Insurance	—Metropolitan Life Ins. Co.
	Insurance	—Penn Mutual Life Ins. Co.
	Coal	—Burlington Northern Inc.
(2)	Coal	—United States Steel Corp.
(2)	Investment	—INA Corporation
	Investment	—Chubb Corp.
	Uranium	—Union Carbide Corp.
	Gas Pipelines	—Panhandle Eastern Pipeline Co.
	Utilities	—Duke Power Company
	Utilities	—Niagara Mohawk Power Corp.
	Oil	—Cities Service Co.
	Oil	—Atlantic Richfield Co.
	Oil	—Continental Oil Co.
	Insurance	—Prudential Ins. Co. of America
	Banks	—Bankers Trust Company
	Banks	—Manufacturers Hanover Trust Co.
	Banks	—First National City Bank
	Banks	—Bank of America
	Utilities	—Public Service Electric & Gas Co.
	Oil	—Standard Oil of California
	Investment	—St. Paul Companies, Inc.
(2)	Banks	—First Bank System, Inc.
(2)	Coal	—Burlington Northern Inc.

STANDARD OIL COMPANY—OHIO

(5)	Coal	—Old Ben Coal Corp.
	Coal	—Republic Steel Corp.
	Insurance	—Metropolitan Life Ins. Co.
	Insurance	—Northwestern Mutual Life Ins. Co.
	Coal	—Old Ben Coal Corp.
	Gas Pipelines	—Consolidated Natural Gas Co.
	Oil	—Marathon Oil Co.
	Utilities	—Detroit Edison Company
(2)	Banks	—National Bank of Detroit
(2)	Oil	—British Petroleum Co., Ltd.
	Oil	—Diamond Shamrock Corp.
	Banks	—Chase Manhattan Bank
	Banks	—Mellon National Bank & Trust
	Coal	—General Dynamics Corp.

TENNECO, INC.

Gas Pipelines	—Midwestern Gas Transmission Co.

TEXACO INC.

Banks	—Cont'ent Ill. Nat. B&T Co., Chicago
Banks	—Northwest Bancorporation
Insurance	—Aetna Life & Casualty
Coal	—Consolidation Coal Company
Coal	—General Dynamics Corp.
(2) Utilities	—Commonwealth Edison
Oil	—Continental Oil Co.
(2) Oil	—Standard Oil Co.—Indiana
Oil	—University Oil Products Company
Banks	—Chemical Bank
(2) Insurance	—Equitable Life Assurance Soc. of the U.S.
Insurance	—Metropolitan Life Ins. Co.
(2) Insurance	—Mutual of New York
Insurance	—New York Life Ins. Co.
Coal	—Burlington Northern Inc.
Coal	—United States Steel Corp.
Foundation	—Commonwealth Fund
(2) Oil	—Amerada Hess Corp.
Oil	—Mobil Oil Corp.
(2) Oil	—Standard Oil Company—New Jersey
Insurance	—Mutual of New York
Banks	—Bankers Trust Company
Banks	—Wells Fargo Bank, Nat Assoc.
(2) Banks	—Chemical Bank
Banks	—Western Bancorporation
Banks	—First Chicago Corp.
(2) Coal	—Union Pacific Railroad Co.
Coal	—United States Steel Corp.
Investment	—Merrill, Lynch, Pierce, Fenner, & Smith, Inc.
Uranium	—United Nuclear Corp.
Utilities	—Consumers Power Co.
Oil	—Cities Service Co.
Foundations	—Rockefeller Foundation
Banks	—Bankers Trust Company
Banks	—Chase Manhattan Bank
Banks	—First National City Bank
Banks	—Dillon. Read, & Co., Inc.
Insurance	—Aetna Life & Casualty
(2) Insurance	—Equitable Life Assurance Soc. of the U.S.
(2) Insurance	—New York Life Ins. Co.
Coal	—United States Steel Corp.

UNION OIL CO. OF CALIFORNIA

(2) Banks	—Bank of America
Insurance	—Prudential Ins. Co. of America
Investment	—Household Finance Corp.
Utilities	—Southern Cal Edison
(2) Oil	—Getty Oil Company
Oil	—Standard Oil of California
Banks	—Western Bancorporation
Insurance	—Mutual of New York
Utilities	—Pacific Gas & Electric
(3) Utilities	—Southern Cal Edison
Utilities	—El Paso Natural Gas Co.
(2) Oil	—Standard Oil of California
Oil Pipelines	—Pure Transportation Co.

UNVERSAL OIL PRODUCTS COMPANY

Banks	—Cont'ent Ill. Nat. B&T Co.. Chicago
Insurance	—Aetna Life & Casualty
Coal	—Consolidation Coal Co.
Coal	—General Dynamics Corp.
(2) Utilities	—Commonwealth Edison
Oil	—Continent Oil Co.
(2) Oil	—Standard Oil Company—Indiana
Oil	—Texaco Inc.
Insurance	Northwestern Mutual Life Ins. Co.
Banks	—Northwest Bancorporation
Banks	—Mellon National Bank & Trust
Coal	—Republic Steel Corp.